The Forgotten Forms of Hindustani Music

The Forgotten Forms of Hindustani Music

Rabindra Bharali

KANISHKA PUBLISHERS, DISTRIBUTORS
NEW DELHI-110 002

KANISHKA PUBLISHERS, DISTRIBUTORS
4697/5-21A, Ansari Road, Daryaganj
New Delhi-110 002
Phones : 2327 0497, 2328 8285
Fax : 011-2328 8285
E-mail : kanishka_publishing@yahoo.co.in

First Published 2008

ISBN 978-81-8457-002-9

PRINTED IN INDIA

Published by Madan Sachdeva for Kanishka Publishers, Distributors, 4697/5-21A, Ansari Road, Daryaganj, New Delhi-110 002. Typeset by Sunshine Graphics, Delhi, and Printed at Nice Printing Press, Delhi.

Dedicated

to

My Parents

Acknowledgements

This book is the outcome of a devoted pursuit in search of knowledge in an area of music that has been long ignored. Quite logically, paucity of information, a relative short list of authentic texts and above all absence of wide expertise were hazards in the research.

The conduct of this scholarly study and the preparation of this book would not have materialised without the valuable guidance, advice and aid of Vidushi Prof. Krishna Bisht. An accomplished musician belonging to the rare genre of traditional school of Hindustani music, Prof. Bisht is an erudite musicologist and a keen observer of the Hindustani music of the time. Despite her hectic schedule as a teacher, scholar and administrator, she was generous to guide and advise me on a subject matter on which few people have competence. It is her scholastic abilities and singular devotion to the cause of Hindustani Classical music which drive the energy and enterprise that she demonstrates on a wide spectrum of activities. Words would not suffice my gratitude to Prof. Krishna Bisht for her invaluable contribution in the completion of this book.

My thanks are due to *Prof. Najma Parveen Ahmad,* Prof. Sunita Dhar, Dr. Manjushree Tyagi for their help and moral support.

I am obliged to Dr. Suneera Kasliwal for her help and constant support in gathering information on the topic.

My thanks are due to Prof. R.S. Bisht, Ustad Iqbal Ahmad Khan, Pt. R.C. Bhatt, Dr. C.K. Jyotishi, Dr. Vijaya Chandorkar for providing a practical perspective of the topic of study.

They kindly entertained my queries and doubts and gave invaluable points of views on the subject matter.

Thanks are owed to Dr. Mohammad Haroon and the Library Staff of the Faculty of Music for helping in collecting information on the topic.

I am indebted to Pt. Deepak Chatterjee and Mukul Shivputra for they have always been my guiding lights as gurus.

I have no words to express my gratitude to my wife Dhriti who gave me every sort of cooperation and inspiration and sustained me during the long period of this work's preparation.

I am thankful to my friend Rajesh K. for helping me in every aspect of the preparation of the book.

AUTHOR

Preface

As we know Dhrupad and Khayal are the two well-known forms of Hindustani Classical music today. Vast and wide studies and researches are always under progress on these forms. But there are lesser known or in the other words the not so popular forms of Hindustani Classical music, which include - Chaturang, Trivat, Ragamala or Raga Sagar, Bamani Sargam or svarsagar etc. It would not perhaps be an over statement to say that these forms are virtually on the verge of extinction.

Having studied classical music under renowned maestros and in a nationally acclaimed institute i.e. the Music Department of Delhi University, I gave serious thought to this aspect and decided to undertake a research study on this subject.

While the study was initiated, historical origin of these lesser known forms were quite obscure. Gradually the long presence of these forms in the history of music began to be revealed.

The book is arranged in five chapters. The first chapter is the historical study of the compositional forms. Here thorough study of the compositional forms from the time of the Vedas to the present period has been done.

The second chapter contains the historical study of the lesser known forms over a span of period extending throughout the age of Prabandha.

The third chapter is the analysis of the lesser known forms from the point of view of present practice.

The fourth chapter deals with the prospects and problems of preservation of the lesser known forms.

In the fifth chapter compositions with notations acquired from different authoritative books and musicians have been presented.

Rabindra Bharali

Introduction

Indian music has been undergoing a remarkable change since very early times. From the historical perspective, Indian music may be divided into three phases : ancient, medieval and modern. The old system of Grama, Murchhana, Jati yielded place to Raga Ragini of modern times. Musical forms underwent tremendous changes. New styles, melodies, types of compositions emerged from time to time and gave rise to modern Indian music.

The relevance of analysis of the compositional forms from the historical point of view is very important because it traces the perspectives and methods of evolution of present trends and aspirations in the role of shaping the future. A systematic, objective and critical study of the compositional forms of Hindustani music based on original source material is still a desideration. It is more evident in the case of lesser known musical forms. The present work is a humble attempt in this direction.

From the significant information available from the texts on music, we can get the idea of the course of evolution of the forms of our music. One can see the gradual rise of gana i.e. grama and desi ragas replacing Jatis. We also get clear picture of the development of the shrutis, swaras, compositions, the connotations of technical terms of music like graha, amsa, nyasa, vadi etc. and even Rasa from the study of the texts.

Vedas are considered to be the earliest extent evidence of our music. After surveying the origin and evolution of the sama scale and Saman, we get the idea about the notes of the fundamental scale which later on became our primary tone system and concept of compositional forms later on.

Bharata's Natyashastra refers to gandharva music as a combination of svvara, tala and pada.

This book contains five chapters. The first chapter gives a brief account of the evolution of the compositional forms. Different kinds of musical compositions were in vogue even at the beginning of the Christian era. They have been described in Bharata's 'Natya Shastra' in connection with the classical dramatic performances. After Bharata, Matang, Parsvadeva and Sharangadeva have described Prabandhas in a systematic and scientific way in their respective works. The period of Prabandha is followed by the age of Dhrupad which reached its height of popularity by the 16th century. With the decline in the appeal of Dhrupad, Khayal took the prime place. In this chapter an intensive study has been made on the origin and development of Dhrupad and Khayal in the light of historical evidence.

Besides these compositional forms, there are lesser known or in other words the not so popular or prevalent forms of Hindustani Classical music, which include the—Chaturang Trivat, Ragamala and Bamani Sargam. It would not perhaps be an over statement today that these forms are virtually on the verge of extinction.

The lesser known forms also have their origin in the Prabandhas. The second chapter deals with the historical perspective of the lesser known forms. To give just a glimpse of their historical background, let us have a glance of the 'Prabandha adhyaya' of 'Sangeet Ratnakar' in the 13th century. Sharangadeva in the fourth chapter gave detailed description of the constituents and varieties of Prabandha. According to him the Prabandhas have four dhatus and six angas. A Prabandha should at least have two dhatus and two angas. In modern times also Dhrupad, Khayal etc. have atleast two parts and two angas. The forms under study have striking similarity with their ancient counterparts. Chaturang as a Prabandha has been mentioned by Matanga in 8th century. Besides this, there are other Prabandha which resemble modern Chaturang, e.g. the four steps of the Chaturmukh Prabandha are sung with svaras, syllabic sound of the musical instruments (pata), verbal text (padas) and auspicious phrases (tena). The modern Chaturang has also four parts, viz verbal texts, bols of tarana (auspicious phrases, tena, which sometimes have meaning), syllabic sound of musical instruments mainly Pakhawaj (pata) and sargam. Similarly the other forms also have their origin in the ancient Prabandhas.

The third chapter is an attempt to analyse the lesser known forms from the point of view of present practice. At present the Chaturang is sung with four angas—Pada, bols of tarana, sargam and bols of Pakhawaj. The Trivat consists of any three elements of the chaturang having patas of Pakhawaj is an integral part. The Raga sagar consists of a garland of ragas. These compositional forms are still in practice in the leading gharanas like Gwalior, Agra, Delhi etc. This researcher was able to collect some compositions from musicians of different gharanas. The lesser known forms also find place in Vaishnav and Sufi music. In Haveli Sangeet tradition forms like Chaturang, Trivet and Ragamala are still in practice.

The history of Chaturang, Trivat, Ragamala etc. is the tale of transition of the well known forms of Hindustani Classical music of yesteryears into the lesser known forms of today. Their journey into unknown is not too distant. So, the revival and the preservation of the lesser known forms are significant. The fourth chapter deals with the prospects and problems of Preservation of the lesser known forms. The measures for preservation are disussed in this chapter. For example, Chaturang, Trivat etc. can be used as the ending piece in a concert like Thumri, Tappa, Bhajan etc. The measures discussed in the chapter are a few of the efforts to preserve lesser known forms. A serious deliberation and initiation of actions to preserve these forms are the demands of the day.

In the fifth chapter compositions with notations acquired from different authoritative books and musicians have been presented.

AUTHOR

[illegible]

[illegible]

[illegible]

[illegible]

[illegible]

[illegible]

Contents

Chapter–1

Analysis of Compositional Forms from the Historical Point of View

Indian music has a very long and unbroken history. Earliest references to compositions were found in the Vedas, the ancient most holy scriptures of the Hindus. There is no written record of the music of Pre-Vedic India. Therefore, the Vedas are considered to be the earliest source of ancient Indian music. The date of the Vedas is supposed to be the 2nd millenary B.C.[1] Of the four Vedas viz Rik, Sama, Yajura and Atharva, the Samveda was rendered musically. Samveda is the starting point of the history of Indian music. Different kinds of musical compositions were in vogue even at the time of the Vedas. In this regard study of different compositional forms of music that have existed from thousands of years ago to the present day is important.

In the Vedic times, the art of music reached an exalted level. The Samagana formed a special feature of the culture of music of that time. The Samagana was of various types with different number of tones in different Vedic recensions (Sakhas) and they had different methods of rendition. Usually three, four or five notes were used in the Samaganas, but in the Kauthuma recension, the Samagana was presented with seven Vedic notes. Thus existence of the svaras in the Samaveda is quite evident. First, there were three Pitch accents, viz. udatta, anudatta and swarita, which later on gave rise to seven notes.

In the "Chhandogya Upanishad' and other works related to the Samveda, references have been found to five fold or seven fold divisions of Samvedic songs called Bhakti-s. The five fold divisions were called 'Panchavidha sama'.[2] These were Prastav, Udgith, Pratihara, Upadrav and Nidhan. There were two additional divisions, which were 'Hinkara and Pranav'. These divisions bore resemblance to the parts of a composition in our Hindustani Classical music like sthayi, antara, sanchari and abhog.

The 'Natya Shastra' of Bharata is an important work for understanding the history of Indian music. The periods of Natya Shastra according to various scholars extended from 2nd to the 4th century A.D. In the Natya Shastra the chapters on music are quite elaborate although the work mainly deals with dramaturgy. Bharata has defined 'gandharva music' as a combination of svara, tala and pada.

Different types of musical compositions have been described by Bharata in his 'Natya Shastra'. He has mentioned seven types of gitakas viz. (1) Madraka, (2) Aparantaka, (3) Ullopyaka, (4) Ovenaka, (5) Rovindaka, (6) Prakari and (7) Uttara.[3] These sapta gitakas originated from the Samveda. The compositions were bound by strict rules of tala. Bharata has also spoken about ancient musical forms like (1) Chandak, (2) Asarita, (3) Vardhamana, (4) Panik, (5) Gatha, and (6) Sama. These compositions were based on permutations and combinations of four talas and three yatis (Sama, gopuccha and srotogata) and three margas (vartika, citra and dakshina).

Bharata has also defined jatis which were the forerunner of ragas. He has divided the jatis into two classes—suddha and vikrita. Again he has mentioned 10 features (lakshana) of jatis, which are graha, amsa, nyasa, apanyasa, audav, shadav, alpatva, bahutva, tara and mandra.

Eighteen jatis have been described by Bharata. In Sangeet Ratnakar, Sharangdeva has described with notations, the distinguishing features of each of the eighteen jatis separately.[4]

In the 32nd chapter of his 'Natya Shastra', Bharata has also dealt with the 'Dhruva' type of musical forms for successful presentation of Natya (drama). The 'dhruva's were 64 in number and were divided into sama and visama.

Dhruva has been defined as:

वाक्य वर्णाह्यलङ्कारा यतयः पाणयो लयाः।
ध्रुवमुन्योन्यसम्बन्धा यस्मात् तस्याद् ध्रुवाः स्मृताः।।[5]

The dhruva is so called because in it words, varnas, alankaras, laya (tempo), yati and Pani-s are regularly connected with one another. There were five aspects of dhruvas: Jati (class), Sthana (occasion), Prakara (variety), Pramana (measure) and Nama (name). The dhruvagiti-s had various aspects viz. Pravesiki, Aksepiki, Naiskramiki, Prasadiki and Antara which had different functions for dramatic performances:

Pravesiki

When actors enter the stage, themes of various rasas were sung. This was called Pravesiki.

Aksepiki

The dhruvas sung for switching over to new mood were known as aksepiki.

Prasadiki

The dhruvas used for bridging the gulf between two successive situations of contrary emotional appeals.

Antara

Antara dhruvas were used to cover the front in the dramas or to smoothen over unexpected sudden incidents like raga, sorrow etc.

In connection with the above mentioned dhruvas, Bharata has discussed about the significance of the Gandharva, constituted out of svara, tala and pada.

Bharata has used the word 'Pada' in the sense of songs to be used in the drama or abhinaya. Bharata has said that the nibaddha type of padas possessed of chanda, yati, aksara etc.[6]

In fact, the Dhruvas were also known as Padas or ancient Prabandhas, accompanied by tala, yati, laya, chanda, rasa and bhava.[7]

'Brihaddesi' of Matanga in the 8th century is a very significant treatise on Indian music. Matanga has mentioned 'gramragas' and these were sung in different giti-s.

Definition of giti:

वर्णाद्यङ्कृता गानक्रिया पदलयान्विता
गीतिरित्युच्यते सा च बुधैरूक्ता चतुर्विधा ।।[8]

The process of singing adorned with varna, alankar etc. associated with pada and layas is called giti. Two varieties of giti-s have been mentioned in shastric texts viz. Padashrita and Svarashrita.

(a) *Padasrita giti:* These kinds of compositions were based on poetic content or text of the song.
(b) *Svarasrita giti:* These were based on musical structure.

Bharata has spoken about four varieties of Padasrita giti-s viz. Magadhi, Ardhamagadhi, Sambhavita and Prithula.[9] In addition to these padasrita giti-s as described originally by Bharata, Sharangdeva has also mentioned five varieties of svarasrita giti-s viz. Suddha, Bhinna, Gaudi, Vesara and Sadharani.[10]

Suddha

Suddha giti is characterized by captivating and straight notes.

Bhinna

Not straight and is accompanied by fine and curved notes taken along with sweet gamakas.

Gauri

This is a quite complicated giti. It consists of movement of notes along all the three registers with continuity and which is characterized by heavy gamakas accompanied by a typical pronunciation of musical notes called 'Ohati'.

Vesara

Vesara or Vegasvara also called Ragagiti by the learned, employs notes in quick succession so as to be delightful in all the four varnas.

Sadharani

'Sadharani giti' is based on the characteristic features of all the four giti-s.

Sharangdeva has discussed both the 'Padasrita' and 'svarasrita' giti-s. It signifies that in Sharangdeva's time both types of giti-s were in vogue.

However, Matanga has mentioned giti-s, associated with ragas for the first time. He described seven giti-s viz. Suddha, Bhinna, Gauri, Ragagiti, Sadharani, Bhasha and Vibhasha. While Matanga accepts seven giti-s, Sharangdeva speaks of only five excluding bhasha and vibhasha. While analyzing the ragas, Sharangdeva also mentioned the significance of composition. In the 'Ragavivekadhyaya' of 'Sangit Ratnakar', he has given the illustration of 'Akshiptika' which was a kind of 'Nibaddha gana' pertaining to 'Margi Sangit'. It was a well-knit musical composition which was sung with the help of tala, svara and pada.

आक्षिप्तिकालक्षणम:[11]

चच्चत्पुटादितालेन मार्गत्रयविभूषिता।।

आक्षिप्तिका स्वरपदग्रथिता कथिता बुधैः।।

The composition was set to one of the marga talas like cacchatputa etc. it was characterized by one of the three margas, which were chitra, vartika and dakshina. It was well knit and well composed with musical notes (sa, ri, ga, ma etc.) and Pada (verbal text). According to Pt. V.N. Bhatkhande all the closed forms of compositions can be compared to Akshiptika.[12]

The difference between Akshiptika and Prabandha is that it is set to desiragas. Prabandha is more elaborate and each Prabandha has many varieties. In Akshiptika there were only three angas viz. Svara, Pada and Tala whereas in some varieties of Prabandha more than three (even six) angas are found. (Incidentally some of the forms under study in this thesis do not come under Akshiptika, as they have more than three parts).

If we look into the history of Prabandha it can be traced back to as early as the 8th century A.D. Matanga's 'Brihaddeshi' is earliest treatise on music which refers to Prabandha. In this treatise Prabandha is found in as a circumscribed form. However, the elucidation of Prabandha as found in 'Sangit Ratnakar' of Sharangdeva is par excellence.

Sharangdeva flourished during the 13th century and wrote the monumental work 'Sangit Rantakar' on Indian music in about 1230 A.D. According to late Thakur Jaidev Singh, "Sharangdeva's 'Sangit Ratnakar' superseded all the previous books on music and has not been superseded by any of the books that followed."[13] Thus, Sangit Ratnakar is considered to be the most important treatise of Indian music 'Sangit Ratnakar' consist of seven chapters. The first chapter, which is called Svaragatadhyaya tells about musical notes, scales etc. The second Ragavivekadhyaya defines and illustrates the various ragas. The third chapter which is called Prakirnaka-dhyaya contains various technical terms of music. The fourth chapter called 'Prabandhadhyaya' which is relevant for our topic of study explains Prabandha and its constituent parts elaborately. In the fifth chapter viz. Taladhyaya treatment of the tala is found. The sixth chapter called 'Vadyadhyaya' pertains to musical instruments. The seventh or the last chapter 'Nrityadhyaya' deals with dancing and acting.

In the fourth chapter, a detailed description of Prabandha is found. Before discussing various types of Prabandha, Sharangdeva defines Prabandha with its minute details,

The definition begins with ganabheda, thus:

"निबद्धमनिबद्धं तद् द्वेधा निगदितं बुधौः
बद्धं धातुभिरङ्गैश्च निबद्धमभिधीयते।"
सञ्ज्ञात्रयं निबद्धस्य प्रबन्धो वस्तु रूपकम्[14]

Briefly this means that gana is two fold, Nibaddha and Anibaddha. Nibaddha comprises 'dhatu' and 'anga' Prabandha vastu and rupaka are the three synonyms terms for Nibaddha.

The part or movement of Prabandha is called dhatu, which is four folds viz. Udgraha, Melapaka, Dhruv and Abhoga. Besides these there is another dhatu called antara between dhruva and abhoga, which is found only in the salaga suda form of Prabandha.

The term Udgraha means the point of lifting or the starting point. The second dhatu is 'Melapaka' which means 'that which joins' and it joins the Udgraha and dhruva. Dhruva is the fixed or the invariable one and it cannot be omitted and hence it is similar to what we call today 'Sthayi'. Abhoga literally means completion i.e. concluding section. In this part the name of the composer or his patron is incorporated.

Prabandha is three fold depending upon the number of dhatus—if there are two dhatus, it is 'dvidhatu', if there are three 'tridhatu', if there are all the four dhatus it is called chaturdhatu. According to Parshvadeva, Melapaka and Abhoga are to be omitted in Dvidhatu Prabandha.

For further clarification Kallinatha may be quoted:

तेन द्विधातुषु प्रबन्धेषु मेलापकाभोगयोः त्रिधातुषु
प्रबन्धेषु सर्वत्र मेलापकस्यैव परित्यागः ध्रुवस्य न
क्वदृपि परित्याग इत्यर्थः[15]

From the above passage it appears that dhruva was of utmost importance and it was never to be omitted.

The inner constituent element of Prabandha is called anga. Anga means limb. Prabandha has been conceived as a Purusha human being with limbs. It is of six kinds:

(i) *Svara:* Sa, ri, ga, ma etc. when they are pronunced (i.e. sung) in their respective pitches are called the svaras.
(ii) *Virdua:* These are the words expressing glory. According to parshvadeva the word 'viruda' has been derived from 'vira'—a word well known in Maharashtra meaning 'opposition'
(iii) *Pada:* Words other than 'Viruda (Viruddha) and Tena which signify meaning came under pada.
(iv) *Tena:* These are the words expressive of the auspicious.
(v) *Pata:* The collection of syllables of musical instruments has been called Pata e.g. dhigi, dhigi etc.
(vi) *Tala:* Cacchatputa etc. or mantha, kanikala etc. are talas. Parshvadeva has called the measure of time and action, tala—talah kalakriya manam.

Thus four dhatus are the basis of Prabandha and six angas form its component elements.

According to the number of angas in a Prabandha there are five jatis, viz., Medini, Anandi, Dipani, Bhawani and Taravali having six, five, four, three, and two angas respectively.

Prabandhas are broadly divided into two groups viz. Aniryukta and Niryukta. Niryukta Prabandhas were governed by strict rules of tala, chanda etc., which could not be altered, whereas Aniryukta had no such rules.

Numerous Prabandhas were prevalent in ancient times, and they were classified under three heads, viz. suda, alisamshraya and viprakirna. They are eight, twenty-four and thirty-six in numbers respectively. There is however another class of suda Prabandha known as salagsuda. The salag sudas are seven in numbers. Maharana Kumbha (author of Sangit Raj) adds 'Mishra-suda as yet another class of Prabandha. According to Kumbha the Mishra suda combines in itself the elements of both suddha and salag suda. Kumbha has described twenty-eight Mishra suda Prabandhas.

One important characteristic of Indian Music is that, new things have always been introduced into the musical forms and this could be one reason why Maharana Kumbha introduced another class of Prabandha, called Misra suda.

Sharngadeva has divided the suda Prabandhas into two classes' suddha and salag. The suddha suda Prabandha has eight types viz. ela, karana, dhenki, vartani, jhambada, lambha, rasaka and ektali. In salag suda variety there are seven types, viz. dhruva, mantha, pratimantha, nihsaruka, addatala, rasaka and ektali.

However certain medieval authors have mentioned the 'Prabandha' in their works, of which we shall now, make a brief survey. In the 14th century a Jain scholar Sudhakalasha authored a book "Sangit Upanishat-Saroddhara". The book was written around 1350 A.D. The work is mainly based on tala and dance, therefore, reference to musical forms is just in passing. One important treatise on music, named 'Sangit Raj' was written by Maharana Kumbha in the 1449 A.D. The book has been divided into five chapters called 'Ratnakoshas' dealing with pathya, gita, vadya, nritya and rasa respectively. In the 'Prabandhollasa' of the gita-Ratnakosha, Kumbha deals with suda Prabandha.[16]

'Sangit Darpan' by Damodar Pandit covers almost every important topic of music. It was written in 1630 A.D. It contains seven chapters and an entire chapter has been devoted to Prabandha some of the Prabandha described by him viz. Surya Prakash, Chandra Prakash, Panchataleswar are also found in 'Ain-i-Akbari'[17] as compositional forms of that time.

Another South Indian work that is relevant in the present context is the 'Chaturdandi prakashika' of Venkatmakhin (1620 A.D.). The material for the chapter of Prabandha has been drawn from his predecessors.

The first 'Kanda' of 'Sangit—Parijat' i.e. 'Raga-gita-Vicharah' contains suda, Alikrama and Viprakirna Prabandhas. It was written by Ahobala (early 17th century). But Ahobala's reference to compositional forms is not elaborate.

Prabandha has also been mentioned by Faqirullah in his work 'Raga-Darpan' as a mere musical form, like dhrupada, etc.

Thus the history of Indian music shows that by and large most of the authors have discussed the compositional forms in their works.

In course of time the structure and the tala of Prabandha became more complex and stereotyped and the form began to decline and disappeared by the beginning of the 15th century.

According to various scholars when the Prabandhas became far too stereotyped and as such lost their popular appeal, then a simplified derivation of Prabandhas emerged in the form of dhruvapada (dhrupada).

The word 'Dhruvapada' is a combination of two words – 'Dhruva' and 'Pada'. Dhruva means any thing which is fixed, permanent or immovable and Pada means verbal text. Therefore 'Dhruvapada' is a song in which the padas or words are well set in a definite structure.

In Dhruvapada both the aspects of gana, nibaddha and anibaddha are manifested. Anibaddha aspects of gana found its expression in the form of alapa and the nibaddha aspects of gana found its expression in the form of Prabandha (composition).

Some scholars are of the view that dhrupad was evolved from its earlier form Prabandha. At what time after Prabandha, dhrupada came into being can only be a matter of speculation. The historical evidence suggests that instead of there being an exact time which can legitimately be ascribed to the genesis of dhrupada there is a long period of transition and a gradual evolutionary process which resulted in the emergence of dhrupadas from their progenitors—the Prabandhas.[18]

A careful study will at once show that 'Dhrupada' was, only an evolution of the 'Prabandha' form of composition. Some scholars are of the opinion that, the dhruva division of the salag suda Prabandha was the ancestor of dhruvapada.[19] According to a general consensus now taking shape among scholars, the salag suda comprising udgraha, dhruva, antara and abhoga comes very close to dhrupada. According to Swami Prajnanananda,[20] the word dhruvapada has been derived from the classical type of dhruva Prabandha, which has been described in the works of Matanga, Parshvadeva, Sharangdeva and others.

As mentioned earlier, Prabandha has been mentioned by Faquirullah as a mere musical form like dhrupad etc. as against its varieties and classes described in Sanskrit musical treatises. To quote Faquirullah: "Prabandha was composed in two movements; it is a musical form in praise of God. In it, there were some traces of Dhrupad, but Dhrupad did not originate from it only."[21]

According to Pt. S.N. Ratanjankar, Dhrupad is purely a legacy of the ancient temple music and the Sanskrit Prabandhas. He states that "Indian classical music has evolved out the religious and temporal folk songs. Dhrupad and Hori, which supposed to be songs of the most pure style of Hindustani Classical music, are adaptations of the temple music employed at the morning and evening services in the temples. In the Tamilian system of music the kirtanams are like the Dhrupad of the north. The difference between the temple music and the Dhrupads, Horis and kirtanams is that while the object of the former is purely devotional, the latter are adapted and modified so as to create a musical effect.[22]

On the basis of the above discussion it is evident that 'Dhrupada' is not an entirely new innovation and it has evolved from the earlier traditional forms, particularly Prabandhas.

The Dhrupada compositions are structured on the framework of Prabandhas. Like Prabandhas, the dhruvapada also has four movements—sthayi, antara, sanchari and abhoga.

In his article "Prabandha and Dhruvapada", "Thakur Jaidev Singh writes,[23] What Dhruvapada did was to combine the idea of the 'udgraha' and 'dhruva' into one and call it sthayi. Like Udgraha, the sthayi is the first movement of the musical piece. It repeats the first few words over and over again which serve the purpose of the dhruva of Prabandha composition. It (sthayi) presents or introduces the raga in its barest outline. Since the idea of Dhruva is already included in the 'sthayi', the 'melapaka' which was meant to join 'udgraha' with the 'dhruva', is dropped and its place is taken by an 'antara', which comes in between the sthayi and the sanchari or abhoga. This is the second movement of musical composition. The sanchari of Dhruvapda has hardly any parallel. The 'abhoga' like the 'abhoga of Prabandha is the last movement of the musical composition.

Dr. Premlata Sharma[24] says, "Although the sthayi of today is accepted to bear the analogy of Dhruva of Prabandha, yet it has to be remembered that Dhruva was supported by a very strong proceeding section called Udgraha which was again sometimes extended through Melapaka, the sthayi of today has no such support and stands on its own. Virtually there are three sections in Dhrupad today, because the last two form one single unit.

And this is true also in the Prabandha system where a vast majority of Prabandhas are composed of three sections. The fourth could be added as Melapaka or Antara, but that was optional in very limited cases. The voyage of 'Dhruva' or 'sthayi' in Dhrupada has a long history both in poetical and musical compositions.

It is interesting to note that most of the characteristics of Prabandha described in 'Sangit Ratnakar' are comparable to that of the Dhrupadas. Just as Prabandha was sometimes dvidhatu, when the Melapaka and Abhoga were dropped, sometimes tridhatu, when Melapaka was dropped and sometimes chaturdhatu, when all the four components were present, even so there are some Dhrupadas which are dvidhatu in which only sthayi and antara are present, some are tridhatu in which only three components, sthayi, antara and abhoga are present. And finally there are Dhrupadas with all the four parts—sthayi, antara, sanchari and abhoga. In the same way out of six angas, three angas—svara, pada and tala are always present in Dhrupada. Similarly 'viruda', 'tenak' and 'pata' can also be used. 'Pata' is already incorporated in 'trivat' form of singing which is a part of study of the thesis.

The forgoing study leads us to the conclusion that Dhrupada was evolved out of Prabandha. No specific mention of dhrupad is available in Sanskrit treatises on music, before the end of the 17th century, with the exception of one reference in 'Sangit Parijat' of Ahobal. Bhavabhatta's definition of dhruvapada in his 'Anup Sangit Ratnakar' is the only one available in Sanskrit treatises on music.

Definition of Dhruvapad as given by Bhavabhatta[25] is as follows:

गीर्वाणमध्यदेशीय भाषा साहित्य राजितम।
दिूचतुर्वाक्यासम्पन्नं नरनार्राकथाश्रयम।।
श्रृङ्गाररसभवाद्यं रागालापपदात्मकम्।
पादान्तानुप्रासयुतं पादान्तयमकं च वा।।
प्रतियादं यत्र बद्धमेवं पादचतुष्ृयम।
उद्ग्राह ध्रुवकामोगेन्तमं ध्रुवपदं स्मृतम्।।

i.e. Dhruvapada is a musical form which is composed in Sanskrit or the language of the middle country. It has two or four sentences. It is based on the affair of men and women and decorated Sringar rasa and the essence of which is infused with raga and alapa. It has anuprasa (rhyme) or Yamaka (repetition of words giving a different meaning each time) at the end of each foot. It has four parts namely Udgraha, Dhruva, Abhoga and Antara.

A distinct point which deserves attention here is that, though the names of the component parts of the dhruvapada has changed since the 15th century, Bhavbhatta in the 17th century has discribed dhruvapada in terms of Prabandha, viz. Udgraha, Dhruva, Antara and Abhoga. This is another proof of the fact that dhruvapada was evolved out of Prabandha.

In the third volume of 'Ain-i-Akbari'[26] Abul Fazl has mentioned that Dhrupad was introduced by Raja Man Singh and his musicians, as a popular style of melody which was approved as the most refined taste and which later "came into universal favor".

We get first historical reference of the modified or rectified dhrupada, in the 15th century. The credit for this goes to Raja Man Singh Tomar of Gwalior. Most of the scholars are of the opinion that dhrupada form was originated by Raja Man Singh of Gwalior.[27] Another viewpoint which deserves consideration is that a sophisticated and complex style of music as dhrupada could not have been the innovation of a single person. It must have taken about hundred years for the development of this style of musical composition before such a great connoisseur of music as Raja Man Singh could extend his patronage to it and took a great interest in its development.

According to Faquirullah, the author of 'Raga Darpan', 'Dhruvapada is a form composed by Raja Man Singh of Gwalior. He composed this style with the help of Nayak Bakshoo, Bhanno, Mahmood, Lohang and Karna.[28] Faquirullah quoted that, Raja Man Singh himself composed many beautiful dhrupadas in such ragas as Savanti, Lilavati, Sadava, Mansahi, Kalyana etc, which are included in 'Man-kotuhal' an important work, which was compiled and edited under his guidance by his court musicologists. Raja Man Singh modified the old shastric form of the dhruvapada Prabandha for its better and wider appreciation keeping in mind the taste and temperament of the contemporary society.

As a compositional structure and as a graspable embodiment of the abstract Raga in its many facets, Dhrupada attained the highest position of respect and glory in Hindustani music as also wide popularity. A few contemporary Persian texts do mention Dhrupad, its form, its popularity and give some biographical accounts of its most famous exponents. As such, these texts deserve a particular study from the point of view of the history of music.

Raga-Darpan, a 17th century work based on Raja Man Singh's 'Man-kotuhal' describes the popularity of dhrupada in the following manner:[29]

"After the innovation of the dhrupada form, the Prabandha style of singing no more remained in vogue. Dhrupada form of singing was so widely accepted and practised by the most renowned as well as common musicians that all other forms of singing disappeared. There are two reasons for these change *(a)* At the time when the dhrupada was taking roots, the margi forms of music were loosing popularity and desi forms of music were being appreciated increasingly. *(b)* Raja Man Singh had assembled together the most renowned musicians two hundred years ago, who had pooled together their vast and rich musical talents—to develop the novel musical form of dhrupada."

In 'Ain-i-Akbari', Abul Fazl has also mentioned, "The dhrupada consists of four rhythmic lines without any definite prosodical length of words or syllables.[30]

The Persian preface of 'Sahasras',[31] the collection of thousand dhrupada texts ascribed to Nayak Bakshu compiled under the order of Emperor Shahjahan (dated C1650), also gives interesting details on the Nayak's dhrupad texts and on the vocal music of the period.

Another interesting account on Dhrupad is found in 'Tuhfat-ul-Hind', a Persian text by Mirza Khan. In Chapter V he has given the description of Dhrupad in the following words - 'It is a composition not in verse but rhymed, it is constituted of four tuks, each tuk is termed differently in this way: first asthai, second antara, the last two are termed as bhog, commonly called abhog and also ahog. It is said that Raja Man Singh was the innovator of this type of song, but the truth is known only to the God Almighty.[32]

According to Ghulam Raza, the author of 'Usalum Naghmat-e-Asifi, "Dhruvapada was a widely prevalent form of singing during the author's time (the latter part of 18th century and the early decades of 19th century). The tuks mentioned are (1) Udgraha, (2) Dhruva, (3) Melapak, (4) Antara, and (5) Abhog.[33]

According to 'Ain-i-Akabri'[34] written by Abul Fazl, the dhrupada style found much encouragement and patronage from the Mughal Emperors. The Mughal Emperor Akbar was a great lover of art and music. During the reign of Akbar, the practice and culture of dhrupada reached their high mark. He collected a number of musicians in his court. There were nine gems in his Court, and Miyan Tansen was the most precious of them all. Tansen, the greatest disciple of the Saint Swami Haridas was the central figure around whom a renaissance of Hindustani music took place. There were many other notable singers and musicians in the royal court out of whom Mian Khuda Baksh, Mian Mansad Ali Khan, Baba Ramdas, Subhan Khan, and Baz Bhadur, the ruler of Malwa were particularly remarkable.

During the time of Emperor Akbar, the dhrupada was sung with four Banis. These were Gobarhar or Gauhar, Khandar, Dagar, and Nauhar. Gauhar Bani originated by Tansen is also called Suddha Bani and is the first one.

The general view is that in Akbar's court there were four musicians named Tansen, Brijchand, Raja Samokhan Singh and Srichand, who hailed originally from Gaur, Dagur, Khandar and Nauhar respectively and the Banis they used were named accordingly.

There is a very popular Dhrupada of Tansen regarding 'Banis' in which he has described the characteristics of each Bani.

बानी चारों के व्यौहार सुन लीजे हो,
गुनीजन तव पावे ये विद्यासार।
राजा गोबरहार फौजदार रवण्डार,
दीवान डागुर, बकसी नवरहार।।[35]

As mentioned earlier, during the Mughal Empire the dhrupad style found much encouragement and patronage. Like Akbar, the Emperors such as Jahangir and Shahjahan were also great Patronage of Dhrupada. There were several musicians in the court of Jahangir. The chief musicians were Bilas Khan (son of Tansen), Makhu etc. Shahjahan was also a great lover of music. He was so fond of Bakshu's Dhrupadas that he ordered a collection of all the genuine Dhrupadas of

Bakshu. This collection is known as 'Sahasras'. (a distorted form of Sahasra rasa). It is a collection of one thousand four Dhrupad songs composed by Nayak Bakshu. Though Aurangzeb is known for his hatred for music, even during his time Dhrupada was popular to the same degree of admiration.

In the beginning of the 18th century A.D. when Muhammad Shah was on the throne of Delhi, Dhrupada was held in high esteem in his court. Music reached the peak of excellence and popularity during the reign of Muhammad Shah. Muhammad Shah earned the title 'Rangile' because of his colourful personality and his love for easy life. He was a great lover of music. Among the names of Muhammad Shah's court musician Niyamat Khan, (Sadarang) is worth mentioning. Niyamat Khan (Sadarang) was a beenkar as well as a Dhrupada singer. Sadarang composed many compositions known as khyals but he himself sang Dhrupadas only.

The foregoing detailed study and analysis of Dhruvapada leads to the conclusion that this form (Dhrupad) occupies the highest rank as a legacy, from the past and attained the highest position of respect and glory in Hindustani Music as also wide popularity.

Khyal is the most popular form in present Hindustani Classical Music. It is a Persian word meaning imagination, conception, thought etc. Khyal is so-called because it is by nature imaginative both in regards of its subject matter and its interpretation.

Controversy rages around the origin of khyal among the scholars. Different views have been expressed in this connection.

Some are of the opinion that Hazrat Amir Khusrau was the originator of khyal and others say that Sultan Hussain Sharki of Jaunpur is to be credited for this style.

According to some scholar's khyal originated from Quwwali style of singing. Some other again argue that khyal was designed after the shastric Akshiptika. In the opinion of some musicologists it has evolved from 'Rupak Prabandha'. Again some others maintain that khyal was created on the image of the Sadharani giti. It has been said by some scholars that khyal is born out of dhrupad just as dhrupad was born out of its earlier form Prabandha.

Hazart Amir Khusrau was a man of many parts. He was a great scholar, warrior, diplomat and statesman, poet and musician and there was hardly anyone to equal him in the medieval period of Indian History.[36] He was one of the most versatile and outstanding musician of the 13th century. An accomplished musician with a creative temperament, Khusrau is credited with a large number of invention and innovations. He is often mentioned as the originator of both Qawwali and Khayal. In her article Dr. Sumati Mutatkar writes: "A versatile genius like Amir Khusrau intelligently introduced Persian melodies into the main body of Indian music. The Qawwali, with its swift passages and elaborations became the forerunner of the fast khayal."[37]

Before the birth of Amir Khusrau in the year 1253 A.D. Qawwali singing was already an integral part of the Sufi cult in India as an instrument of worship and as an expression of devotional fervour. With his many faceted creativity and high musical imagination, Amir Khusrau infused the Qawwali with a new complexion and shape, making its singing very much more musical, attractive and imaginative. With an added Indian ethos Qawwali became more conducive to spreading all over the mystic message of the Sufis. This Qawwali gave rise to a form of singing in the shaping of which Amir Khusrau seems to have made a substantial contribution.[38]

It is to be particularly noted that Amir Khusrau mentions all his musical innovations in his works, wherein Khayal as a musical form does not find a place. The word Khayal is found as a figure of speech. In the 'Ain-i-Akbari' khayal is conspicuously missing. In his article Thakur Jaidev Singh writes:[39] "After two hundred years of Muslim rule, Sanskrit words were mostly forgotten by the musicians, though they know the practical art fairly well. The word Khayal became popular and was naturalized, Amir Khusrau did not invent the style, he simply gave the Arabic name to it. Some element of the art of Qawwali singing may have erupt into the indigenous style, but it has been so wonderfully assimilated that it is impossible to disentangle it."

However some khayal compositions supposed to be Amir Khusrau's are still prevalent. It appears that at the initial stage these compositions did not assume the name 'khayal' and were popular among the Qawwals.

Sultan Hussain Sharqui of Jaunpur was also a great patron and connoisseur of music. The authors of 'Sarmaya-Ishrat', 'Marifun-Naghmat', 'Madnul-Mousiqi' and many other writers are of the opinion that, Sultan Hussain Sharqui was great master of the art of music and he was the founder father of khayal style.[40]

According to Pt.V.N.Bhatkhande: "It is not correct to believe that any single person could have originated and developed the khayal style. It is likely that musical compositions similar to khayal already existed in the society, but they did not have due reorganisation and appreciation by the people at that time. Later in the fifteenth century Sultan Hussain Sharqui took a fancy for it and encouraged the musicians to sing in this style, which might have given impetus to its development and popularity."[41]

Swami Prajnanananda was also of the view that khayal was much improved and better understood during the time of Sultan Hussain Sharqui.

The credit for the efflorescence of the khayal goes to Sadarang (Niyamat Khan) and Adarang (Feroz Khan) who flourished under the regime of Muhammad Shah Rangile. Renowned exponents of dhrupad and vina, Niyamat Khan (Sadarang) and his nephew Ferozkhan (Adarang), musicians at the court of Muhammad Shah Rangile devised a slow moving structure for Khayal, retaining the raga features and stateliness of dhrupad, particularly freeing it from rhythmic rigidity.

It is indeed strange that although Niyamat Khan (Sadarang) is today famous as the originator, propagator and prolific composer of hundreds of khayals which are popular to this day, he never sang them himself, nor did he teach them to any member of his family. This must have been due to the snobbish attitude of the Dhrupadiyas of those times who looked down upon other forms of classical music.

Judging from different viewpoints it can be said that khayal could not have been the innovation of a single person, we may also take into consideration the fact that ancient shastric texts contain the root of khayal.

In 'Sangeet Ratnakar' some styles of singing have been described, the structure of which resembles the khayal style. Such as 'Akshiptika'. According to Sharangdeva, Akshiptika is made up of svaras, padas and sung to one of the marga tala, chachatputa. In the opinion of some musicologists, it embodies all the elements of khayal i.e. svara, tala and pada. The other forms also contain these elements. So this view is not tenable.

Khayal has also been compared to Rupak Prabandha by some scholars. As mentioned earlier Prabandha, Vastu and Rupak are the three synonyms for Nibaddha.

About Rupak Sharangdeva has said that, a Rupak acquires novelty by employing new Ragas, new tonal and verbal structures, new talas, tempo and specific compositions. From the description it is understood that the Rupak Prabandha is a musical composition, which is novel and original in conception. The new forms of composition, rhythm, tempo etc. are designed with different metres and aesthetic sentiments and moods.[42]

Some musicologists are of the opinion that khayal was created on the image of the Sadharani giti because various embellishments permissible in Sadharani giti are employed in Khayal. According to Sharangdeva Sadhari giti was a style which combined within itself the excellent features of all the other four types of giti.[43]

Thakur Jaidev Singh is of the opinion that khayal form of song is a natural development of the Sadharani giti along with the bhinna giti.

Apart from these views there are another view that, khayal is born out of Dhrupad just as dhrupad was born out of its earlier form Prabandha.

According to Acharya Brihaspati Khayal is a mixture of dhrupad and Qawwali. He says, as some characteristics of Dhrupad are found in khayal, it is also known as 'Langra Dhrupad.'[44]

Dr. Sumati Mutatkar writes in his article, "Akbar's reign is considered to have been the golden age for dhrupad, since the rulers were generally speaking not conversant with Sanskrit and with the traditions, symbol and imagery of Hindu mythology a general in difference to its devotional character and an ignorance of the literary aspect of music gradually developed among the musicians. As a result the Dhrupada lost much of its vigour and started to become stereotyped. The only direction in which further development seemed possible was that of tonal structure or abstract music in which words were of no special importance. In this process the khayal evolved from Dhrupad."[45]

In Dhrupada the lyrics are extremely high and their development inside the strict tala circle is of great importance. The khayal singer can take full freedom so far as his 'Khayal' or imagination and has scope for many vocal embellishments. Dhrupada gradually lost its popularity and had to give way to khayal.

On the basis of the above discussion and various view-points, regarding the origin of khayals, it is evident that khayal could not have been the innovation of a single person. It is likely that musical compositions similar to khayal were already in existence.

Khayals are composed in North Indian languages. The text of most khayals are in Braj Language, and next to it in

Rajasthani, Punjabi and some in Hindi also. The object of description can be anything. But Khayals containing eulogies to kings, description of Nayikas of Shringar rasa situations and marriages are the most popular now. In this there are only two sections—sthayee and antara.

There are various gharanas of khayal singing and style of singing varies from one gharana to another. The main gharanas of khayal singing are—Gwalior, Agra, Rampur Sahaswan, Kirana, Delhi, Patiala etc.

Besides the compositional forms which have been discussed in this chapter, there are also other forms of Hindustani Classical music which are lesser known today. The lesser known forms of Hindustani Classical vocal music, viz Chaturang. Trivat, Bamani sargam and Raagmala will be the subject of study in the following chapters.

REFERENCES

1. Vidushi Krishna Bisht, 'Sacred Symphony', p. 9.
2. Paranjape, 'Bharatiya Sangeet ka Itihas', p. 72.
3. Paranjape, 'Bharatiya Sangeet ka Itihas', p. 70.
4. Sangeet Ratnakara (Adyar Edn.), Vol. I.
5. Natya Shastra, Chap. 32.2.
6. Natyashastra, Chap 32, Verses 23-30.
7. Prajnanananda, "A Historical study of Indian Music', p. 56.
8. Sangeet Ratnakar, Vol. I, Verse 14.
9. Natya Shastra, Chapter 32, Verse 23-30.
10. Sangeet Ratnakar, Vol. II, Chap.I, Verse - 2-7.
11. Sangeet Ratnakar, Vol. II, Verses 25-26, p. 21.
12. Dr. Manjushree Tyagi, 'Significance of the Compositional Forms in Hindustani Classical Music', p. 11.
13. Dr. Thakur Jaidev Singh, 'Indian Music', p. 110.
14. Sangeet Ratnakar, Vol.II, Chap.IV, Verses 4-5.
15. Commentary of Kallinatha in 'Sangeet Ratnakar', Vol.II, p. 205.
16. Sangit Raj, p. 577.
17. Abul Fazl, 'Ain-i-Akbari', Allami, Vol.III, Eng. Trans by Jarrett, p. 265.

18. Prajnanananda ,'A Historical Study of Indian Music', p. 181.
19. Dr. Sumati Mutatkar, 'Dhrupada: Its Legacy and Dynamics (an article)- Aspect of Indian Music', edited by Dr. Sumati Mutatkar.
20. Prajnanananda, 'A Historical study of Indian Music', p. 181.
21. Faqirullah, 'Raga Darpan', p. 38.
22. Commemoration volume - An article by M.S.N.Ratanjhankar, p. 210.
23. Thakur Jaidev Singh, 'Prabandha and Dhruvapada' Journal of the Indian Musicological Society, September 1976, pp. 9-10.
24. Dr. Prem Lata Sharma (Article), 'The Dhruva in 'Dhrupad' - Dhrupad Annual', 1987, p. 118.
25. Bhavabhatta - 'Anup Sangeet Ratnakar', Svaradhyaya, p. 47.
26. Abul Fazl, 'Ain-i-Akbari', Allami, Vol.III, Eng. Trans. From the original manuscript by H.S.Jarrett, p. 265.
27. Faqirullah - 'Raga Darpan', Hindi Translation, H.N.Dvivedi, 'Man Singh Aur Mankutuhal', p. 91.
28. Faqirullah - 'Raga Darpan', p.39 of the manuscript.
29. Faqirullah - 'Raga Darpan', pp. 38-39.
30. Abul Fazl - "Ain-i-Akbari" Allami, Vol.III, Eng. Trans. From the Persian, by H.S. Jarrett, pp. 265-266.
31. 'Sahasras' edited by Dr. Prem Lata Sharma, Hindi trans. pp. 8-13.
32. Prof.Najma Perveen Ahmad, 'Hindustani Music', p. 95.
33. Usulun—Naghmat-e-Asifi, pp. 131-132.
34. Abul Fazl, 'Ain-i-Akbari', Eng. Trans. By Blochman, pp. 681-682.
35. Marif-un-Naghmat, Part-II, p. 17.
36. Mirza Waheed, 'The Life and Works of Amir Khusrau', p. 79.
37. Dr. Sumati Mutatkar, 'Evolution of Indian Music', Lakshya Sangeet, June 1956, pp. 2-3.
38. Sushil Mishra, 'The Khayal - Aspect of Indian Music', p. 85.
39. Thakur Jaidev Singh, 'The Evolution of Khayal', Commemoration, Volume, p. 132.
40. Pt. V.N. Bhatkhande - 'Bhatkhande Sangeet Shastra', Part-I, p. 55.
41. Pt.V.N. Bhatkhande,'Bhatkhande Sangeet Shastra', Part-I, p. 55.
42. Sangeet Ratnakar, Vol. II, Chap II, Verses 3-7.
43. Thakur Jaidev Singh - "The Evolution of Khayal", p. 128.
44. Achrya Brihaspti, "Musalman Aur Bharatiya Sangeet.
45. Dr. Sumati Mutatkar, 'Evolution of Indian Music', Lakshya Sangeet, 1956, pp. 2-3.

Chapter–2

Historical Perspective of the Lesser Known Forms

A study of the genesis of the lesser known forms logically leads us to the age of Prabandha. The forms to be studied are Chaturang, Trivat, Bamani Sargam or Svarartha and Raagmala or Raagsagar. It is to be seen whether these forms have remnants of the ancient Prabandhas. The study begins by examining one Prabandha after another in search of these forms in them in different musical treatises starting from the 'Brihaddeshi' of Matanga.

Chaturang

Chaturang is sung with four angas—Pada (verbal text), the bols of tarana, Sargam (solfa syllables), and finally the patas of mridangam or Pakhawaj. In certain Chaturang a text in some other language is sung.

The Chaturang Prabandha has been popular since Matanga's time (8th cent.) Matanga in his 'Brihaddeshi' has mentioned Chaturang Prabandha for the first time. According to him:

रागताल चतुष्केण यत्र भाषा चतुष्टयम्
गीयते गीत चतुरैश्चतुरङ्गः स उच्चते।।[1]

i.e. Its four sections are sung in four ragas, four talas and four languages. In today's Chaturang the four angas and four sections need not necessarily be there. But the composition is set to one raga and one tala. So, the Chaturang Prabandha of

Matanga has no resemblance with modern Chaturang. But mention of Chaturang as a musical form in the 'Brihaddeshi' establishes the fact that the name is more than twelve hundred years old.

Chaturang Prabandha has also been mentioned by Pandit Mandali in his 'Sangeet Shiromani' (1429). To quote him:

विरूदं तेन्नकश्चतत् द्वयं शरभलीलके।
नेष्यते गीतविद्विस्तैः तेनासौ चतुङ्गकः।।[2]

Chaturang Prbandha as mentioned by Pandit Mandali also does not bear any similarity to modern Chaturang.

The most Voluminous Sanskrit work on music, viz. Sangeeta Raja was written in the fifteenth century. The work is attributed to Nripati (Rana) Kumbhakarna (1433-1468). It is an outstanding work on the three fold art of music and Rasa. The book has been divided into five chapters called Ratnakoshas dealing with Pathya, Gita, Vadya, Nritya and Rasa respectively. Each of the above chapters has four divisions or Ullasa; further four subdivisions of each Ullasa are called 'Parikshanas'. The fourth Parikshana of the Prabandhollasa is on prakirna Prabandhas and Rana Kumbha has enumerated Chaturang Prabandha under this. Chaturang Prabandha has been elaborately discussed from sloka nos. 66 to 71.

उदग्राह ध्रुवकौ यत्र पृथक् द्विद्विदिलौ तथा।
अमोगस्तु पदैरन्यौः पाटैश्चैव स्वरास्तथा।।
विरूदानि च तेनास्व चत्वारः क्रमतः पृथक्।।
x x x x x x x
भिन्नाश्यां रागातालश्यां चतुरंङ्ग प्रबन्धके
ध्रुवोन्तरार्द्धतालादिराभोगस्तेन–मोक्षणः[3]

'Sangita Samayasara' is another unique and elaborate work on music and dance. It is attributed to Parshvadeva, a Jain scholar of 13th century. Sangita Samaysara contains nine chapters called adhikaranas on vocal music, instrumental music and dance. The fifth adhikarana contains description of Prabandhas and Chaturang is one of the Prabandhas named therein.

प्रबन्धस्तेन्नकरणं स्वतेतापियुतः स्मृतः
तेपासपयुतः प्राज्ञैश्चतुरंङ्ग इतीरितः।।[4]

i.e. The Prabandha tenakaranam has svara, tena, tala and viruda. Chaturang comprises tena, pata, svara and pada.

However in most of the later works on Indian music including 'Sangeet Ratnakar' of Sharangdeva, Chaturang as a Prabandha is conspicuously missing.

Ghunyatu'l Munia which was written in 1374-75 is a unique Persian work on Indian Music. The original text happens to be the earliest of any Persian works on Indian Music. The name of the author is unknown. Ghunyatu'l Munia may be placed almost next to the 'Sangeet Ratnakar', in chronological significance. The text deals with the profound art of Sangita comprising Gita, Vadya and Nritya. It is in two parts, divided in four chapters and 18 sub-divisions.

While discussing various forms of ancient Prabandha gities, the author has mentioned Chitarang (Chaturang) form of Prabandha. According to the author, Chitaranga is a kind of Prabandha like Chaturmukh, the difference being that every music part of the later is made up of svara, pata, pada and tena and the same are sung in a particular varna, while in Chitarang (Chaturang) all the four parts are rendered in four ragas, four talas and four languages, the raga, tala and language of each part being different.[5]

Dasopant (1551-1615), a Marathi poet and composer used to compose a Prabandha a day, some of which have been published. Among them there is a Chaturang Prabandha.

Chaturang Prabandha of Dasopant in Raag Dhanashree:

मनि भरल्ला अवधूत रे ।रे। सक्लेप्सिहितु आदि गुरू।
शरीर संगपरगे शशि शीतल अखंडितु बो
सुवा सीत दतु सजाशोभितु गंधे करूनि चर्चितु बो,

अनंता सुखते दितु मुक्तावलि यथा उरी,
किरिटादि अलंकारी दिनभाती विफल्लु जाला,
अरे। उपमाने गेली लया।।
सा सा नि पा नि सा पा नि सा गा गा गा सा नि ना सा
नि नि नि नि पा गा गा मा पा नि सा सा नी पा मा गा मा
पा सा गा पा सा मा गा सा मा गा सा गा गा पा गा मा पा नि पानि
सा मा गा सा नि सा पा सा नि नि नि पा मा गा मा
पा नि सा सा नि पा मा मा गा सा । छ ।।
झेम झेम ज्ग ज्ग झक्क किणरा कक्क कु धांधांधारि तकु
झेन्तं झेन्तं झक्रिागा दाम् दाम् तद्धिमि धिमि धिमि धिमि
दिग्दां दिग्दां धाड़ा धाड़ा
तद्धिमिकिटाथड़ी कुनंक किरगा।। छ ।।[6]
तेन्न तेन्ना तेना तेन्ना तेन तेना तेन्ना तन्ना तेना तेन्ना
तेना आरे तेना तेन्ना तेन्ना तेन्ना तेन्ना तीन तेना तेना
तीन तीन तेना डुती डुननेन्नातेना।। धा ।।

While discussing Prabandha 'Matanga' in his 'Brihaddeshi' has mentioned another Prabandha called 'chatuspadi', which is quite similar to modern Chaturang. According to Matanga:

यत्र प्रतिपदार्थ तु गीतं तालयुक्त भवेत्।
स्वर तेनक संयुक्तोः सा चतुष्पादिका भवेत् ।।[7]

i.e. Where the song is endowed with meaning in every unit of text (pada) with tala, having svara, and tenaka, that is chatuspadika.

Now, if we analyse modern Chaturang from the point of view of ancient Prabandha, then, Chaturang, consists of five angas and not four, viz—svara, tena (bols of tarana, which is sometimes meaningful) tala, pada and pata (syllabic sound of musical instruments). Nowadays tala is an essential part of a composition and hence, it is not considered as an anga.

Now, we can compare Chaturmukh Prabandha of Sangit Ratnakar with modern Chaturang. Sharangdeva describes the

Chaturmukh Prabandha under Viprakirna class.

स्वरैः पाटैः पदस्तेनैर्वर्णौः स्याय्यादिभिः न्कमात।।
चत्वारश्चरणा गेया ग्रहें न्यासश्चतुर्मुखे।।
इति चतुर्मुख प्रबन्ध।[8]

i.e. The four steps (padas) of the Chaturmukh are sung with solfa notes (svaras), syllabic sound of musical instruments (Pata), verbal text (Pada) and auspicious phrases (tenas). It ends in Udgraha. Chaturmukh Prabandha has also been mentioned by Rana Kumbha in his 'Sangeet Raj'. He describes Chaturmukh as a variety of Viprakirna Prabandha and is quite similar to that of 'Sangeet Ratnakara's'.

Chaturmukh Prabandha has also been mentioned in some of the pre-Ratnakar work's. "Manasollasha" by Someshwara III is an encyclopedic Sanskrit work. The work was written in 1129 A.D. Someshwara has been frequently quoted by Sharangdeva as an authority of Indian music. The work is divided into five parts of twenty chapters (Vimshati), each dealing with various subjects such as science of Polity, Lore of taming horses and elephants, architecture, iconography, painting, music and dance, games etc. Someshwara has referred to the Chaturmukh Prabandha in the following verse:

स्वरैश्चैव तथा पाटैस्तेन्नकैश्च तथार्धाकृम्।
न्कमणैव चतुर्मागो गीयते स चतुर्मुखः।।[9]

Haripala in his 'Sangeet Sudhakar' (1175) has also mentioned Chaturmukh Prabandha and the description is as follows:

चतुर्मुखस्वरैः पाटैः पदैस्तेन्नैर्निबध्यते।
स्थाय्यादिभिस्तथा वर्णैराभोगोऽन्ते पदान्तरेः।
ग्रैहर्न्यासो विधातव्यो भवेदेधं चतुर्मुखः।।[10]

In fact the above description of Chaturmukh Prabandha confirms the fact that in the twelfth century, Chaturmukh

Prabandha was sung with four angas viz, svara, pata, pada and tena. It resembles modern Chaturang undoubtedly.

In most of the works where Prabandha has been described, Chaturmukh Prabandha finds place. These ancient Prabandhas whose names do not convey the use of four fold angas are similar to modern Chaturang in content.

We can compare modern Chaturang with 'Varnasvar' Prabandha of Sangeet Ratnakar. Sharangdeva has described 'Varnasvar' is a variety of Ali Prabandha. He quote him:

स्वरैः पाटैः पदैस्तेने रचना वाच्छितक्रमात।।
यस्य स्यान्तेनकैर्न्यासः स वर्णस्वर उच्यते।
स्वरादेराविन्यासभेदादेष चतुर्विधः।।[11]

i.e. The Prabandha, that is composed with svaras, patas, padas and auspicious words (tenakas), placed in any order at will is called 'Varnasvara'. It is four-fold according to the distinction of the svaras etc. being the first part of the composition.

Varna-svara Prabandha has also been mentioned in Matanga's 'Brihaddeshi'. According to Matanga:

निबद्धो हस्तपाटैर्यः संयुतस्तेनकैः पुनः।
स्वरैः पदश्च पाटैश्च तेनकैश्च समन्वितः।।
गीयते तालपुक्त यः स वर्णस्वरकः स्मृतः।।[12]

i.e. That which is composed with patas of the hand and is again combined with tenakas, is combined with svaras, padas, patas and tenakas (and) is sung in combination with tala, that is known as Varna-svara.

Both the Prabandhas, Chaturmukh and Varnasvar have been elaborately cited by Maharana Kumbha in his 'Sangeet Raja'. In the tritiya Parikshana of Prabandhollasa both the Prabandhas are enumerated under Alikrama Prabandhas.

Parshvadeva, in his 'Sangeet Samaysara' has also spoken about both the Prabandhas viz–Chaturmukh and Varnasvar in sloka nos. 55 and 56 of the fourth Adhikrana.

स्वतापितेसहितो जयश्रीरिति कीर्तित:
स्याद् वस्तु विजयश्रीश्च वर्णस्वर चतुर्मुखै।।
स्वपापतातेसहिता विज्ञेया गीत कोविदै:
प्रबन्धो वर्धानानन्दस्तथा हरविलासका।।

Parshvadeva states that Varnasvar and Chaturmukh comprise svar, pata, pada, tala and tena.

The south Indian work that is relevant in the present context is the 'Chaturdandi Prakashika' of Venkatamakhin (1620 A.D.). The material for the chapter of Prabandha has been drawn from his predecessors. Both the Prabandhas Chaturmukh and Varnasvara have been mentioned in sloka nos. 159 and 135 respectively and the descriptions are quite similar to that of 'Sangeet Ratnakara'.

Sahasrasa (Sahasra rasa) is a collection of one thousand dhrupad songs by Nayak Bakshoo in the seventeenth century. This collection was compiled in accordance with the directives of Emperor Shahjahan. Although, 'Sahasrasa' does not contain any composition like Chaturang, reference to Chaturang has been made.

चतरंज अंक इन, ताकौ ब्यौरो पुछत कोटिहि रूप धुवा रच्यौ।
निरत अंग मे समझ देख धौं विचार, कौन सब्द, कौन निसब्द के वच्यौ।।[13]

According to Dr. Prem Lata Sharma, the editor of the Published Sahasrasa, चतरंज in the above verse stands for Chaturang.

Raag Kalpadrum which was written in 1842 by Krishnananda Vyas contains thousands of compositions of different forms of North Indian music. Along with other compositional forms, Chaturang also finds place. Here is one example of Chaturang, found in Raag Kalpadrum.

Chaturang in Raag Paraj, taal-teentaal.

चतुरंग गायन गाइये रिभाइये रधुनायको स्वर तान
ताल सों राग डाट सो स्वर सम सो मान मनाइये।

तननन नूं द्र द्र तूं तदीम तदीम नादर दर द्र द्र द्र
द्र द्र द्वं तनूम उद तद्रनुं द्रतनूं यलल यललललूं लाइये।।
सानिध प न ग रे सा सा रे ग ग म म प प ध ध नि नि सा सा
प सा सा प सा धाइये।
सप्तस्वर तीनग्राम एकईश मूर्च्छना गुणीजन सममान
ज्ञान पाय परस पाइये।।[14]

Wajid Ali Shah, who was born in 1822 was a great lover of music and literature. He, himself composed ghazals and thumris under the pen name of 'Akhtar piya'. He has the credit of writing many books including the two 'Najo' and 'Wani' on Hindustani music. In 'Najo' he has cited many compositions of different musical forms. He has devoted a whole chapter for Chaturang. In the fifth chapter 'Sada-e-Panjum', he has cited many Chaturangas. One of them is given below.

Chaturang in Raag Aalheiya Vilabal, Taal–Teen Taal.

Sthayee

चतुरंग कों भेद जो गुनी जानत वादी सुर सों।
सक्षम सुर सों ठीक तान कर न्यारो गावो

Antara

बड़ो ग्यान वा को रंगीली
जो सुर को पहचाने हो
सरेगा रे म ग रे सा मा गा मा गा रे सा
धड़तिक धड़ंग तक
तु ना धा तु ना धा
तु ना तु ना कर नक तक तक धा[15]

Trivat

Trivat is sung with any three of the four angas of Chaturang, having Pata (syllabic sound of musical instruments) as one of the integral parts. So, Trivat consists of any two of the angas of Pada, Sargam and bols of tarana and pata, which is never to be omitted.

Now, let us compare the modern Trivat with that of ancient Prabandha. Indeed, we have obtained many Prabandhas having three parts and thus sharing similarity with modern Trivat. In 'Sangeet Ratnakar' we find a Prabandha called 'Tripatha', which is a variety of Viprakirna Prabandha having some similarity with modern Trivat. Triptha has been described by Sharangdeva as:

पादत्रयं त्रिपथके पाटैस्य विरूदैः स्वरैः।
इति त्रिपथप्रवन्धाः।।[16]

i.e. Tripatha has three steps (Padas) (composed respectively) with the syllabic sound of musical instruments (patas), Panegyrics (birudas) and solfa notes (svaras).

Again, we find a Prabandha called Trivangi, which has been popular since Matanga's time. Matanga in his 'Brihaddeshi' has mentioned Trivangi Prabandha. According to him:

पदैः स्वरैस्तथा पाटैर्वृन्तत्रयपदेन च
तालत्रयविमिश्रेण त्रिभङ्गिरभिधीयते।।[17]

That which is composed with padas, svaras, patas with feet in three metres mixed with three talas is named Trivangi.

Trivangi Prabandha has also been described by Sharngadeva. His description goes like:

खरैः पाटैः पदैरूक्तस्त्रिभङ्गिः स च पञ्चघा ।
एकस्त्रिभङ्गितालेन वृन्तेनान्यस्त्रिमङ्गिना।।

i.e. Trivangi is said to be composed of solfa notes, syllabic sound of musical instruments (Patas) and padas and is fivefold viz (1) Sung with Trivangi tala, (2) Composed in Trivangi metre, (3) Sung with three talas, (4) Sung with three metres, (5) Sung in the propitiation of three gods. It ends with two cycles of tala.

Someshwara in his 'Manasollasha' has also spoken about Trivangi Prabandha. According to Somesha:

भिन्नवृन्तैस्त्रिभिः पादैः स्वरपाटसमन्वितैः
तालत्रयनिवन्धाश्चत् त्रिभङ्गिरभिधीयते।

Trivangi Prabandha also finds place in Parshvadeva's 'Sangeet Samayasara'. In sloka no. 54 of the fourth Adhikaran, Parshvadeva speaks like:

स्पितापयुता तज्ज्ञैर्हयलीला निगद्यते।
पपाटास्वर्युतौ जेयास्त्रिभङ्गि चोभयात्मिकौ।।[18]

i.e. Hayalila has svara, viruda, tala and pada, Trivangi comprises Pada, Trivangi comprises Pada, Pata, Tala and Svara.

Trivangi Prabandha has also been mentioned by other writers like Haripala, Somraja etc.

In the South Indian work 'Chaturdandi Prakashika', by Venkatamakhin, Trivangi Prabandha also finds place. It has been discussed in sloka nos. 186 to 193.

So, Trivangi Prabandha also bears some similarity to modern Trivat form of singing.

Trivat as a form, has been mentioned in many of the works of seventeenth century or later.

'Raag Darpan' by Faqueerullah is one of the monumental works which was written during the seventeenth century. The manuscript was written during Aurangzeb's time. It was based on Raja Man Singh's 'Man-Kotuhal'. 'Raag-Darpan' consists of ten chapters and the fourth chapter deals with description of svaras and different forms of Hindustani music. In this chapter Faqueerullah has mentioned 34[19] types of musical forms, which were popular during his time. Among these 34 types of forms, Trivat also finds place. Following are the forms described by Faqueerullah.

1. Suraj Prakash
2. Chandra Prakash

3. Shruti Bhadra
4. Raag Kudum or gram
5. Jhoomra
6. Swar Adrutni
7. Prabandha
8. Man
9. Dhruvapada
10. Qual
11. Dhruva
12. Chutkala
13. Sadhar Chutkala
14. Qual
15. Tarana
16. Khayal
17. Naqsh
18. Qalbana
19. Nigar
20. Tillana
21. Sohela
22. Baseet
23. Vishnupad
24. Trivat
25. Kane
26. Lachari
27. Gujri
28. Katarkha
29. Sadra
30. Bol-leela
31. Tappa
32. Mankal
33. Bar
34. Zakri

'Tohfat-Ul-Hind' is another important work, written during Aurangzeb's period. The name of the author is Mirza Khan. The author has mentioned different types of forms and styles of singing prevalent in his time. The author has divided the forms into two parts.[20]

1. These styles and forms which were popular and practised during ancient and medieval periods. These styles were in the Prakrit language. These were of seven types : *(a)* Geet, *(b)* Jhoomra, *(c)* Chhand, *(d)* Dhruva, *(e)* Mantha, *(f)* Dhruva, *(g)* Prabandha.
2. Those forms which were popular during the authors own period : *(a)* Dhruvapada, *(b)* Trivat, *(c)* Phoolbandh, *(d)* Jugalbandh, *(e)* Vishnupad, *(f)* Khayal, *(g)* Qual, *(h)* Tarana, *(i)* Jakri or Zakri, *(j)* Kadhka, *(k)* Bagad, *(l)* Baad or Bar.

It is to be noted that Trivat is second in sequence after Dhruvapada, which perhaps establishes its superiority to other forms. So, it is evident that the Trivat form of singing was prevalent during the 17th century and was equally popular as dhrupad and khayal.

Historical account of any musical form would be incomplete without having a glance at the vernacular literature and collections of compositions of great musicians. We may cite a few examples which will prove beyond doubt that Chaturang and Trivat, etc. were practised along with other major forms like Dhrupad. In the following Pada of Baiju, these forms have been mentioned:

1. गीत नाद की असावरी धुरपत परवंधा
   तुपक त्रेवट तिलाना चतुरंग
   प्यारे सोहत भूपर।।
   कहे बैजू नायक उन्क्र जुन्क्र की
   वजीर मन राजा राज करत
   हरि को ध्यान धरे।।

2. धारू धुरपद प्रबंध छंद
   गीत गुनी मात्रा चतुरंग त्रेवट निषनी
   देस विदेस
   भाषा संस्कृत बितेरव
   क्हे वैजु वावरे सुन हो गोपाल नायक

हिरन बुलावे पाहन पिगलावै
तेरी लाख मेरीएका।।[21]

Now most authors place Baiju as a senior contemporary of Tansen. At one place Baiju has been named as one of the following eight disciples of Swami Haridas : Baiju, Gopal Lal, Madan Raya, Ramdas Dwivakar Pandit, Som Pandit, Tanna Mishra, Raja Sauka (Soura) Sen.

Similarly in compositions of Tansen these forms have been mentioned.

1. नाल चारू धोवा माठा पर माठा चतुरंग जबू राग जल
वैंत पारसी छंद रज्यो
शत जंजाल त्रेवठ राग चंगी संगीत दारू तानन
गज बांस दांस भुमरा गोता भरत।
तिलानां कोतवोल ध्रुवपद वजीर
प्रबंध की निसानी
तानसेन कहे रासो अगम जाको पार
न पायो रचपच हारे

2. नाद नगर बसायो सुरपति
हीरा पै पाट नग लगें खरज जंजीर
त्रेवट कुँजी नामें ध्रुवपद
सो नग छिपाये।।
जौहरी मीयां तानसेन गाहक
जलालदीन जिन याको
कोल कीनों अकवर पारखी पायो।।[22]

In the 2nd composition, "Miyan Tansen metaphorically presents himself as a jeweller, his customer being none, other than Akbar his patron. Dhrupada—a precious stone has been kept in a locked place which is to be opened with the key (Trivat). Thus the superiority of Dhrupad is evident. At the same time, it is clear that Trivat (as also Chaturang) was an established form of singing in the 16th century.

Gopal Nayak, who was a musician of all India fame in the time of Alauddin Khilji and was contemporary to Amir Khusroo also mentioned Chaturang and Trivat in his Pada. In the following Pada of Gopal Nayak different compositional forms have been mentioned.

सुर प्रथम सा रि ग म नाद रे, ताहै प्रगट वेद रे।
धारू ध्रुपद संगीत प्रवंध छंद ग्रनी गावत शेष रे।।
चतुरंग त्रेवट तेलाना सप्त सुरन कौ भेद रे।
कहे नायकगापाल सरेगम अगम सुर देख रे।।[23]

To conclude the historical survey of Chaturang and Trivat it can be said beyond doubt that these two forms have known in Indian music for more than 12 hundred years Rich both in content and form, they have always been in vogue.

Bamani Sargam or Svarartha or Svarsagar

Bamani is an Urdu word which means 'with meaning'. Ba = with, Mani = meaning. Bamani Sargam is a type of composition, made up of the solfa syllables (Sa, re, ga, ma etc.). The Solfa syllables are so arranged that these become meaningful. These kinds of compositions are still sung by some of the artistes of Gwalior gharana and they term these compositions as svar-sagar.

Now, if we look back to the age of Prabandha, we find a similar Prabandha called svarartha. Matanga in his 'Brihaddeshi' has mentioned 'Svarartha Prabandha' for the first time. According to him:

वाच्छितार्थस्वैरेव यत्र सभ्यक् प्रगीयते
वस्त्वान्मकेषु गीतेजु स स्वरार्थ इति स्मृतः।।[24]

i.e. Where the song is properly accomplished with the svaras (solfa syllabus) yielding the desired meaning, that is known as svarartha among the song made of vastu.

Someshvara in his 'Manasollasa' has referred to Svarartha as a full fledged Prabandha. First he explains the meaning of svarartha saying that in this Prabandha svaras themselves express the desired meaning:

स्वराक्षराणि सङ्गृह्य वच्छितार्थो विरय्यते।[25]

Someshvara also provides us with an example:

सम (मा)गमागम (मा)पापमादम (पाप) धानि (निसमागम:)[26]

Sharangdeva in his 'Sangita-Ratnakar' has mentioned Svarartha Prabandha as a variety of Ali-Prabandha. His description goes like:

यत्र स्वराक्षरैरेव वाच्छितोऽर्थोऽभिधीयते।
स रवरार्थो द्विधा गुद्धो मिश्रस्तै: गुद्धमिश्रितै:।।
ग्रहन्यासोऽस्य भुयोऽसौ सप्तधैकादिकै: स्वरै:।
क्रमोत्क्रमाभ्यां बहुशो भिद्यन्तो द्विस्वरादय:।।[27]

i.e. Wherein the desired meaning is expressed through the note names themselves, that is Svarartha. It is two fold, viz. Suddha and mishra (composed) with standard and mixed notes. It ends in graha. Again it is sevenfold viz (composed) with one to seven notes. Of these the bi-tones and others are further divided into many varieties by the alternation of their order.

Maharana Kumbha, in this 'Sangit Raja' has also spoken about Svarartha Prabandha. In the third parikshana of Prabandhollasa, Rana Kumbha has enumerated svarartha in the Alikrama Prabandha.

यत्र वाग्गोयकारेण स्वरै: षड्जादिसादिकै:
अर्थे निवघ्यतेऽभीष्ट: स स्वरार्थो निगद्यते।।[28]

The description of svarartha Prabandha by Rana Kumbha is quite similar to Matanga's.

However, the description of Svarartha Prabandha in 'Sangit Samayasara' of Parshvadeva differs from Matanga and Kumbha. According to Parshvadeva:

गीयन्ते पदतालाभ्याममी गीतविशारदैः।
स्वरार्थस्ता(पि) सैर्ज्ञेयः स्यात् तथा सिंहविक्रमः।।[29]

i.e. These are sung with pada and tala. Svarartha should be known as having svara, tala and viruda so as Simhavikrama.

In the South Indian work 'Chaturdandi Prakashika' of Venkatamakhin (1620 A.D.) svarartha Prabandha has been described under Taravali jati of Prabandha. According to the ancient classification of Prabandhas depending on angas, Tarvali jati means dvi anga (consisting of two angas) Prabandha.

Interestingly Poet Bihari's Satsai (17th century) contains some 'dohas' with meaningful sargams. The poet has not used the word Bamani or Svarartha. Bihari was an outstanding poet of his time, patronized by the ruler of Amer (Jaipur) Raja Jaisingh (1617-1667). A few examples may be cited here:

1. सुनि पग धुनि चितइ इतइ नेहाती दियेही पीथि
2. पग पग मग अगमन परत चरन अरून दुति झुलि

The above examples clearly establish the fact that Bamani sargams were well known in the seventeenth century.

Material found in Sanskrit granthas cannot, always conclusively prove that a certain form or Raga was prevalent during the period of its writing. Because Sanskrit authors have always been tradition bound.

Thus, to prove the prevalence of anything, vernacular-references have been helpful.

'Raag Kalpadrum', which was written in 1842 by Krishnananda Vyas contains these types of compositions, e.g.

Raga—Bhairav, Taal—Dhamar Bahar
Maga Madha mere magare dhanisama resani
Paga mere dhare dhare paga dhama dhamare sasa resani
Sare gama mere sagare maga mere dhama dhama pai padhani

Sadha sadha paga dhare sada pai mori[30]
Neka na mani

In this composition, except 'neka' all the other syllables denote the svaras of Bhairav raga. A meaningful composition is thus made up of only solfa syllables.

Raga Mala

This is a very attractive song form. As is evident from the name it consists of a garland of ragas in which sections of the song are sung in several ragas one after another, but tala is the same from beginning to the end.

Although, compositional form, named Raga Mala was not prevalent during the age of Prabandha, we find another Prabandha called Raga Kadamba which bears similarity to Raga Mala.

Sharangdeva in his 'Sangit Ratnakar' has elaborately described Raga Kadamba. It is a variety of Ali Prabandha.

रागकदम्बप्रबन्धाः
नन्द्यावर्तः खस्तिकश्च द्विधा रागकदम्बकः।
चतुर्वृन्तश्चतुस्ताले रागराजिविराजितः।।
नन्द्यावर्तो भवेत्तस्य तालमानद्वुयन वा।
उदग्राहेणाथवा न्यासौ गद्योनैनं परे जगुः।
तालेनैकेन केचित्त, खस्तिको द्विगुणस्ततः।
अब्जपत्रोऽब्जगर्भश्च भ्रमराम्रेडिते मते।।
केषांचित् पूर्वपूर्वस्माद द्विगुनः स्यात् परः परः।[31]

i.e. Raga Kadamba is two fold viz. nandyavarta and svastika. Nandyavarta is composed of four vrittas set to four talas and is embellished by a series of ragas. Its completion is done with two cycles of tala or with Udgraha. Other, however hold that it may be composed in prose and some others say that it is set to one tala only.

The commentator of Sangita Ratnakar, Kallinatha states that, Bhramara—a variety of Raga Kadamba Prabandha was sung by Gopal Nayak which consisted of a chain of twelve ragas and twelve talas.

Rana Kumbha in his 'Sangeet Raja' has also described Raga Kadamba elaborately. In the third Parikshana of Prabandh-aollasha, Kumbha enumerated Raga Kadamba in Ali Krama Prabandha.

यत्र स्युर्भूरयो रागाः स स्याद रागकदम्बकः ।
नन्द्यावर्त्तः खस्तिकश्च पझपत्रस्तृतीयकः

x x x x x x x

कश्चिद गद्येन रचितं तालेनैकेन केनचित् ।
नन्द्यावर्त्ताभिधं प्राह नानारागविराजितम्।।[32]

Rana Kumbha's description of Raga Kadamba is almost similar to Sharangdeva's.

Parshvadeva in his 'Sangeet Samayasara' has also mentioned Raga Kadamba but the description is very indistinct. According to him:

जयमालाचक्रवालौ तथा रागकदम्बकः
कलार्णवो झोम्बटश्च रासकश्चोभयात्मिका।।[33]

i.e. Jayamala, Chakrabala, Raga Kadamba, Kalarnava, Jhampata and Rasaka are Ubhayatmika.

Faqueerallah, in his Raag Darpan has mentioned one singing form called Rag Kudum along with other forms which were popular in his time. The form Raag Kudum must have come from Raga Kadamba as the names are quite similar. We can assume that Raga Kudum is a distorted form of Raga Kadamba.

Abul Fazl in his 'Ain-i-Akbari' has mentioned Raga Kadamba as a form of songs. He mentioned 7 types of song forms. These are: (1) Surya Prakash, (2) Pancha Talesvara, (3) Sarvatobhadra, (4) Chandra Prakash, (5) Raga Kadamba, (6) Jhumra, (7) Svaravartani.[34]

Raga Kadamba Prabandhas, are compositions consisting of a garland of ragas had never fallen into disuse. Only the name changed. Instead of Raga Kadamba it came to be known as Raga Sagar or Raga Mala. References to such compositions are found in the works of Swami Haridas, Tansen, Baiju etc. One of Baiju's Raga Sagar begins with Bhairavi and contains more than thirty ragas. Along with common ragas, it has rare ragas like khat, lachari, bahaduri, Deepak etc. The following ending line clearly indicates that the composition was meant to be sung in the form of Raga Sagar.

बैजू बावरा रावरी हितु तिहारी राग सागर
गावत तिल तिलक सिर मांफ देखाल[35]

In Vaishnava Sampradaya such compositions are found in abundance.

In Islamic tradition a type of songs called 'Sokhwani' is sung during the Moharrum. Beautiful Raga Mala compositions are found in these type of music. No instrument is used during the Moharrum being a mourning period.

REFERENCES

1. Brihaddeshi of Matanga Muni, Vol. II, edited by Prem Lata Sharma, p. 217.
2. Bharat Kosha, Compiled by M. Ramakrishna, p. 197.
3. 'Sangeet Raj' by Maharana Kumbha, Edited by Dr. Prem Lata Sharma, p. 615.
4. Sangeet Samayasara, edited by Acharya Brihaspati, pp. 101-02.
5. Ghunyatul's Munia, Eng. Trans. By Shahab Sarmadee, p. 49.
6. M.B. Dhond-Prabandha, Dhrupad tatha khyal, Sangeet Kala Vihar, April 1975, p. 17a.
7. Brihaddeshi of Matanga Muni, edited by Dr. Prem Lata Sharma, p. 211.
8. Sangeet Ratnakar, Vol. II, Eng. Trans by Dr. R . K. Shringy, p. 297.
9. Manasollash by Someshwar, p. 121.
10. Bharathosha, compiled by M. Ramakrishna, p. 199.
11. Sangeet Ratnakar, Vol. II, Eng. Trans. By Dr. R. K. Shringy, p. 266.

12. Brihaddeshi of Bharat Muni, Vol. II, edited by Prem Lata Sharm, p. 241.
13. Sahasras, edited by Dr. Prem Lata Sharma, p. 29.
14. Rag Kalpadrum by Krishnananda Vyas, Vol. II, p. 30.
15. Najo, Wajid Ali Shah, p. 42.
16. Sangeet Ratnakar, Vol. II, Eng. trans. Dr. R.K.Shringy, p. 282
17. Brihaddeshi of Bharat Muni, edited by Prem Lata Sharma p. 217.
18. Sangeet Samaysara of Parshvadeva, K.C. Brihaspati, p. 102.
19. Raga Darpan, Original Manuscript, p. 41.
20. Hindustani Music by Dr Najma Perveen Ahmad, p. 39.
21. Acquired from Prof. K. Bisht.
22. Acquired from Prof. Krishna Bisht.
23. Acquired from Prof. Krishna Bisht.
24. Brihaddeshi of Matanga Muni, edited by Prem Lata Sharma, p. 239.
25. Manasollasha, Someshwar, p. 101.
26. Acquired from Vidushi Krishna Bisht.
27. Sangeet Ratnakar, Vol. II, Eng. trans. by R. K. Shringy, p. 278.
28. Sangeet Raj edited by Dr. P.L. Sharma.
29. Sangeet Samayasara, Edited by K. C. Brihaspati, p. 101.
30. Raga Kalpadrum, 1st Part, p. 86.
31. Sangit Ratnakar, Vol. II, Eng. Trans. By R. K. Shringy, p. 228.
32. Sangeet Raja, Edited by Dr. Premlata Sharma, p. 595.
33. Sangeet Samayasara, Edited by K. C. Brihaspati, p. 100.
34. Ain-i-Akbari, Vol. III, p. 266.
35. Acquired from Prof. Krishna Bisht.

Chapter–3

Analysis of the Lesser Known Forms from the Point of View of Practice Today

Although the forms—Chaturang, Trivat, Bamani Sargam and Raag Mala are lesser known today, still they are prevalent. All these forms of vocal music are still performed by some of the traditional artistes. In this chapter, it will be the endeavour to present a full-fledged study of these forms in the context of present day performance.

Chaturang

Chaturang Prabandha as described by Matanga in the fifth century contained four parts, but each of the parts was rendered in different ragas, talas and languages. The Chaturang Prabandha in the 12th century also had four parts, but there was only one raga and one tala. There were four angas also viz - Pada svara, tena and pata.

The modern Chaturang is also composed with four angas but four parts need not necessarily be there.

Chaturang can be of different types, depending upon its constituent parts and their arrangements. Here is an example of Chaturang, in which four angas are sung in two parts. The first part consists of Pada and Sargam and the second part is sung with Patas of Pakhawaj and bols of tarana.

Chaturang in Raag Bhupali

पायल बाजरी बाजरी मोरी

झनक झनक झन रून झन ननन
ग ग प धा सां सां
सां रें गं गं रें गं गं रें सां
एसन चतुरंग बनाये।
धागे टुंग, धागठुंग, धागे केट केट धागे
धागे ठुंग धागे ठंग, ठंग, ठंग, ठंग,
तनन तनन तन नन ननन।[1]

In most of the Chaturangas, the sthayee is sung with pada, and the rest of the three angas viz. tarana, sargam and patas constitute the second part, which can be considered as antara. Here is an example of this type of Chaturang.

Chaturang in Raag Bihag, Tala–Jalad Trital:

सुरज्ञान ले तिरवट अक्षरसों गावत चतुरंग
नि़ सा ग म नि प म म ग म ग सा सा नि़ नि़ सा नि़।
प म प सां स ग म प नि नि सांनि प म ग सा म म ग सा
ना द्र द्र तुं द्र द्र द्र द्र तुं तुं तनन तन नि तत द दा निकड़धान।
किती कड़न कतक धुमकिट तक् गिदिगन धागेनग।
तिरकट तक धुमकिट तक धेत् ड़ाङ्ग कड़ा धा धीं ता धा।

In some Chaturangas along with the sthayee the first part of the antara is also sung with pada. A Chaturang of this type is cited below:

Chaturang in Raag Marwa, Teen Taal.

चतरंग सब मिल गाइये, गाइये बजाइये और रीझाइये।
मोहम्मदरा वरकाज सोहाग नाचत सब मिल देदे तारी
सा ग म ग रे सा छोम्छन ननन छोम्छननननन,
तकधी तक धी तक तिर किठ तक धी कड़ां धा धा ती धा धा।[2]

In certain Chaturaagas, a text in some other language is sung in place of the patas. An example of this type of Chaturang is given below, wherein place of the patas of Pakhawaj, two lines of Persian language are found.

Chaturang in Rag Jaunpuri Teen Taal:

चतरंग रससन गाइये
ले जानिये सुर लाल पर
आलाप कर सुनाइये।।
नाद्रि धितिलानं तदीं दीं तननन
नितारे नितारे तादीं दीं
सा सा सारेम रेमप मपध
म प धा नि प धा नि धा नि सां
हाषवे गुयौ कि फर्दा तर्कनु सत किनौ
वाजचु फरदो सुफर युयो जरा दुनिंया कुनौं[3]

Mostly Chaturangas are sung in Khayal style in medium tempo. In all the leading gharanas of Khayal, viz - Gwalior, Agra, Rampur, Delhi etc. Chaturang is in practice and is a part of their talim. We can cite one example of chaturang, which is sung by the artistes of Gwalior gharana.

Chaturang in Raag Des, Teen Taal:

चतरंग को गावे रस रौंगत सों
कर तीवर कोमल देखभाल कर
तर तीवर अति कोमल सुरसों न्यारो न्यारो सुरसंगत सों
दिर दिर दिर ता ना ना दिर दिर ता नो म्तान्ना दिर दिर
तुं दिर दिर दिर दिर दिर दिर दिर दिर दिर दिर दानि।
उनं चास कोट तान तिनके कठीन रंगीले हे ब्योरे।
म म प प नि नि सां सां रें सां नि ध प म
धा किट तक धुम् किटतक धिन्ताक धिन्ताक धिन्ता
किड़नग न ग धिरिं किटितक तक धी किड़ तगं तघ्डान् तक धा।[4]

In Delhi gharana also the Chaturang is very much in practice. According to Ustad Iqbal Ahmed Khan, the Khalifa of Delhi Gharana, modern Chaturang form of singing is the innovation of Amir Khusrau. Here is an example of Chaturang which according to Ustad Iqbal Ahmed Khan is a composition of Amir Khusrau.

Chaturang in Raga Paraj, Teen Taal:

चतुरंग को बनाये सुध मत सों
सम्पुरन सुर गुनी तीवर गाये
ग म गम पर ध मं प धनि धनि सांरें नि सां
रें गं रें गं रें सां नि सां धनि सां रे सांनि ध प
धा किटतक धुम किटतक धुम किटतक धुम किटतक
धुम किटतक तृक धाकिट धा धुम किट तक धा
क्ड़ां धा क्ड़ां धा क्ड़ां धा

If we analyse the constituent parts of this Chaturang, it consists of only three angas, viz—Pada, Sargam and Patas of Pakhawaj. The bols of tarana are conspicuously missing.

The great musicians and musicologists of modern times have also given emphasis to Chaturang form of singing. Late Pt. V N Bhatkhande has included Chaturangas in his Kramik Pustak Malikas. Many Chaturangas are found in different volumes of the Kramik Pustak Malikas with notation. Late Pt. Vishnu Digambar Paluskar, one of the greatest vocalists and musicologists of Gwalior gharana was famous for his rendition of Chaturangas. He himself composed many Chaturangas. One of his Chaturangas in Raga Sindhura is cited below:

Chaturang in Rag Sindhura, Teen Taal:

चतरंग गावो गुनि सब मिलकर
आज तान आलाप करन सो
नादिर धितिलान तदीं दीं तननन
सानिध प म ग रे सा रे म प धा सां
सप्तस्वरास्त्रयो ग्रामा मूर्च्छना द्विकविंशती तान रयकोन पंचाशत्
इत्येतत् स्वरमंडलम्।।[5]

Chaturang has also been composed by many of the modern time composers. Here is an example of Chaturang composed by Vidushi Sumati Mutatkar, an exponent of Agra and Gwalior style.

Chaturang in Raag Charukeshi, Teen Taal:

दिर दिर तनों तान्ना देरेना तदारे दानि
ना दिर दानि तुं दिर तन देरेना तदारे दानि
तदियाना रे तदारे तारे दानि तारे दानि
तारे दानि तद्र दाानि
ना दिर दिर तदारे दानि तुं दिर दिर तदारे दानि
नदीं दीं तननन नदीं दीं तननन, धा धा किटतक धा
किट तक धामु किट तक गदिगिन, तिट कत
गदि गिन धा, तिट कत गदि गिन धा, तिट कत गीद गिन धा
गाइये चतुरंग, उपजे रसरंग, सुमधुर
सुर अंग, राग ताल संग सारे गम प ध नि सां
रें सां नि सां नि ध प प
हर शिव रांकर, जय गंगाधार
अरधांगी गौर्रा, सुचारूकेशी त्वमेवशरणं
भव भय हरणं, नमामित्वां नमामित्वां।[6]

One speciality of this Chaturang is that the Pada comes in the third section of the composition.

Forms like Chaturang are also found in Vaishnav music. In Haveli Sangeet tradition which is still alive in the temples of Mathura and Vridanban, Padas similar to Chaturang are sung. The following Padas of Krishnadasjee resembles Chaturang form of singing.

Raag Yaman:

लाल संग रास रंग चल मान रसिक रमन
ग्र ग्र ता ग्र ग्र ता त्त त्त त्त त्त त्त त्त त्त थेहे गति लीने।।
स रि गम प ध नि ग म प धा नि, धानि सुनि ब्रजराज।
राजकुवर लावतरी अति गति यति भेद सहित।।
ताननि नांन न न न न न न अति अनि आस लीने।।[7]

In this Pada we find all the four components of Chaturang, viz – Pada, Pata, Sargam and bols of tarana.

Trivat

'Trivat' is sung as a form of Hindustani Classical music in Khayal style. Trivat is also prevalent among the Kathak dancers. In vocal music it is generally sung as a short piece in the pattern of chota khayal. The name 'Trivat' itself indicates that this form is composed of three variegated elements. In short, Trivat can be defined as a variety of song having three of the four elements of a Chaturanga, but the Patas of Pakhawaj should always be there. It has different varieties. Here is a variety of Trivat, which is composed of Pada, bols of tarana and Patas of Pakhawaj.

Trivat in Raag Bihag, Taal Teen Taal:

धड़ी पल छिन गुनी गावे त्रिवट को
गावे बजावे रिझावे सरस्वती को
ना द्र द्र तुं द्र द्र द्र द्र तुं तुं त नं न न न न
कड़धान किती कड़न कतक धुमकिट तक् गिदिगन धागेनग
तिर किट तक धामुकिट तक धांत् कड़ान धा ताधा ता धा।।[8]

Another variety of Trivat, which is composed of bols of tarana, sargam and patas of Pakhawaj is cited below:

Trivat in Raga Jaijaiwanti, Teen Taal:

दिर दिर तनन तन देरेना दीं तों तन देरेना
तदानी तन ननन देरेना तन ननन
देनी देनी तदानी
उदतन देरेना दी तन देरेना
तन दरेना तन देरेना तन देरेना
रे गा रेसा निसा धनि रे गरे
पम धप निध
किड्धेत् नागिन धागी तिरिकिटतक
तान धा धा तिरिकिट तक् तान धा धा
तिरिकिट तक तान धा धा।।[9]

Although Trivat consists of three elements, we have found Trivat with lesser elements too. Here is a Trivat, which is obtained from Raag Kalpadrum of Krishnananda Vyas having two elements viz Pada and Patas of Pakhawaj.

Trivat in Raag Paraj:

ऐय ऐय एय ऐयां धा धिलांगता धिधि कु कु भ्फाइये।
धिकिटित ध्रत न थुंन थूंनं मृदु मृदङ्ग मिलाइये।।
परन प्रति प्रति पधति मन उडति यदुराइये।
पढ तराना पराक्रम प्रेमरङ्ग त्रेवट सुनाइये।।[10]

Here is another example of Trivat which is composed of two elements, i.e., Patas and Pada.

Trivat in Raag Bhoopali, Teen Taal:

धिरिकिट तक् धी धी ना धीना ती तीना धीना
धी धीना धी धीना थुं थुं नाथुं थुं थुं थुंथुं किडनग
गुरूको गावे तब वेद पावे गुनी,
धिरिकिट तक् धिरिकिट तक् धाक्डान् धा धा धा
तगड् झगड् तक् थुंना।।
द्रुत मघ्य विलबीत और ताल काल सम विषम को
कंठबरन कर दिखावे सुध मत तब बड़ो गायक कहावे
धिरिकिटतक् धिरिकिट तक् धाक्डान् धा धा धा
नगड् झगड् तक् थुंना।।[11]

The Trivats which are found in Pt.V.N.Bhatkhande's Kramik Pustak Malikas are also composed of two elements viz bols of tarana and patas of Pakhawaj. The following Trivat is composed in this manner.

Trivat in Raag Hamir, Ektaal: [12]

दिर दिर दिर दिर दिर दिर तोम, दिर दिर तोम्तोम तनन नन, नातादरे दानि ना दिर धिल्लान् दिर दिर धिल्लान् तुं दिर दिर दिर दिर दिर दिर दिर दिर दिर

Antara-I

यललि यललि यललोम् यललोम, यला यलालल्ले देरेना दिम् तदानि
तननन नननननन

Antara-II

तत्ता धिं धिं थुं थुं धिं धिं धा धा तिर किट धुमकिट तघ्डान तक् धित्लान्
तद्धा धिगिन्न धा धा तिरकिट धुमकिट तघ्डान् तक् धित्लान् तद्धा धित्लान
तद्धा धित्लान तद्धा

There are certain Trivats, which are composed of patas of Pakhawaj only. So, modern Trivat can be defined as a variety of song, in which Patas of Pakhawaj is highlighted mainly. Here is a variety of Trivat, which is composed of patas of Pakhawaj only.

Trivat in Raag Adana, Teen Taal:

क्डां धा धा धा धा किटतक गदिगन धा
धा किटतक धुम किटितक गदिगन गदिगन धुमकिट
तकिततका किट तक धुमकिटतक गदिगन नगतिट
क्डां धा कडां धा कडां धा।।[13]

Antara:

धा किटतक धुमकिट तक गदिगन गदिगन धुमकिट
तकिटतका किट तकधुमकिटतक गदिगन नगतिट
कडां धा कडां धा कडां धा।

The above cited Trivat is sung by the artistes of different gharanas. According to Ustad Iqbal Ahmed Khan of Delhi gharana, this Trivat is a composition of Amir Khusrau.

Trivat of this type can be compared to Kaivat Prabandha of Matanga, which was also composed of Patas only.

Trivat form of singing is in practice among the artistes of different gharanas. Here is an example of Trivat which is a composition of Agra Gharana.

Trivat in Raag Kedar, Teen Taal:

Sthayee

तिरकिट तक धे धेन्ना धगीनधा धाधातुना।
धगीनधा धाधातुना धगीनधा धाधातुना।।

Antara

धा किटतक धुम किटतक धित्ता धा।
शुकरंग क्डां क्डां धाधाधा
क्डां क्डां धाधाधा
क्डां क्डां धाधाधा[14]

The great composers of modern times also have given emphasis in Trivat form of singing. Late Pt.V.D.Paluskar himself composed many Trivats. One of his Trivats is cited below:

Trivat in Raag Sohini, Teen Taal:

Sthayee

देर्ना देर्ना देर्ना तन देरेना
तन तुंदिर तदरे दानि तदानी
उदनित तन देर्ना देर्ना देर्ना

Antara–I

न दिर दिर दिर तुं दिर दिर दिर
थ्दर दिर दिर दिर दिर दिर दिर दिर
नि रे गम गरे निरे सानि धनि धमध
धिरि धिरि कत् धिरि धिरि किट तक्
तक्डान् धिरि धिरि किटतक तक्डान्
धादी कत् तकिट धा, धिरि धिरि किट तक
तक्डान् धादि कत् तकिट धा, धिरि धिरि
किटतक तक्डान् धादि कत् तकिट धा।।

This Trivat is composed of three elements, viz bols of tarana, sargam and patas of Pakhawaj.

In Vaishnav Sampradaya whose mode of worship is full of music, songs like Trivat find place. The following pada of Shree Govindjee, which is sung in Haveli Sangeet tradition resembles Trivat form of singing.

'स रे ग म प ध नि आलाप करत रस उपजत तान सरंग
निर्तत मत जत लेत ग्र ग्र त त त किट धिम क धिलांग
धोंग वाजत मृदंग "गोविन्द"[15]

The above pada consists of three elements of Trivat, viz. pada, Saregama and Patas of Pakhawaj.

Here is another example of this type, in which is composed of pada, patas and sargam.

Composition in Raag Hamir, Taal–Dhamar

गावत ताल धमार गुनिजन सवमिल
सखि संग आवत धावत,
गावत मांगत सार गुनिजन।
धुमकिट तक धुमकिट तक धा धा कंड़ा, धा धा कंड़ा
ताथै ताथै तिरकिट धा
सरिसा गमधा नि ध सां रें सां नि ध सां[16]

Raagmala or Ragasagar

Raagmala is a prevalent form of Hindustani Classical music. This form of music is used in both vocal and instrumental music. Earlier, dhrupad singers used to perform dhrupad Raagmala, but nowadays it is rarely heard. But Dhrupad style Raagmalas are still extent especially in the Vaishnav Sampradaya.

Raagmala consists of a garland of ragas and is also known as Raagsagar i.e. ocean of ragas. Raagmala is sung in Karnatak style of music also and is very popular. Text of one Raagmala is given below as an example:

Sthayee **Taal – Ektaal**

गान लच्छन जनरंजन छायालग रागनसो।
जव गुन सो रट रट प्रभु श्याम लच्छन मारग को।।

Antara–I

व दिन कामोद प्रथम, मंत्री आरंभी गान।
सुर सुर के संकर सो दरबार में गावन को।।

Antara–II

ध्यान धरत जलधर के बह्मा अरू सरसुति के।
वागीश्वरी गुनन खान आनंद के सुरनन सो।।[17]

The sthayee of the above Raagmala is composed in Raag Janaranjani, Chaya, Sorath and Shyam as underlined. The first antara is composed in Raag Kamod, Arabhi, Shankara and Darbari and the second antara is composed in Raag Jaladhar, Saraswati, Bageshree and Aanandi.

To understand the different ragas used in the Raagmala the notation of the Raagmala has been given below:

Sthayee: Tala Ektala

प	–	प	ध	म	म	म	म	प	–	प	–
गा	ऽ	न	ल	छ	न	ज	न	रं	ऽ	ज	न
X		0		2		0		3		4	
प	रे	रे	ग	म	प	ग	म	रे	रे	सा	–
छा	ऽ	या	ऽ	ल	ग	रा	ऽ	ग	न	सो	ऽ
X		0		2		0		3		4	
रे	रे	म	म	प	–	नि	नि	सां	नि	सां	सां
ज	ब	गु	न	सो	ऽ	र	ट	र	ट	प्र	भु
X		0		2		0		3		4	

(Contd.)

नि	रें	नि	नि	म॑	प	म	रे	नि़	सा	रे	म॑
श्या	ऽ	म	ल	छ	न	मा	ऽ	र	ग	को	ऽ
X		0		2		0		3		4	

म	रे	प	म॑	प	–	गमप	गम	रे	सा	रे	सा
वा	ऽ	दि	न	का	ऽ	मो ऽऽ	ऽ ऽ	द	प्र	य	म
X		0		2		0		3		4	

रे	–	म	–	प	–	ध	–	नि ध	ध	नि	प
मं	ऽ	त्रो	ऽ	आ	ऽ	रं	ऽ	भि ऽ	गा	ऽ	न
X		0		2		0		3		4	

नि	ध	सां	नि	प	–	ग	प	नि	(सां)	नि	–
सु	र	सु	र	के	ऽ	स	ऽ	क	र	सो	ऽ
X		0		2		0		3		4	

						म		सा	(सा)		
नि॒	प	सां	–	नि॒	प	ग॒	म	रे	रे	मा	–
द	र	बा	ऽ	र	में	गा	ऽ	व	न	का	:
X		0		2		0		3		4	

Antara (2)

म	–	म	म	प	प	सां	सां	ध	ध	म	–
घ्या	ऽ	न	ध	र	त	ज	ल	ध	र	के	ऽ
X		0		2		0		3		4	

म॑	प	नि	ध	म॑	प	रे	रे	रे	रे	सा	–
ब्र	ह्म	ह्म	ऽ	अ	रू	स	र	मु	ति	के	ऽ
X		0		2		0		3		4	

म	ग॒	म	–	नि॒	ध	नि॒	सां	नि॒	सां	–	सां
बा	ऽ	गे	ऽ	श्व	री	गु	न	न	खा	ऽ	न
X		0		2		0		3		4	

ग	–	म	ध	प	–	रे	रे	सा	सा	ग	म
आ	ऽ	नं	द	के	ऽ	सु	र	न	न	सो	ऽ

The modern time composers also compose and sing Raagmala. The following Raagmala is composed by late Pt. Balvant Rai Bhatt, who was a great exponent of Gwalior gharana and was a disciple of Pt. Omkarnath Thakur.

Sthayee

बेलरिया हरी झुकी रही अतही प्यारी मनभाई रे बलमा

Antara

बाग बाग में नन्हे नन्हे उमगे पतवा, नयी तयी कलियॉ
खिली वहुरंगी,
प्यारी, भावरंग के मन भाइरे बलमा।[18]

The above Raagmala is composed in raag Adana, Nat, Kedar, Bahar, Malavkaushik, Malgunji and Sohini. Although the names of the ragas are not mentioned in the lyrics of the composition, the composer has termed it Raagmala, as it is composed in different ragas.

Late Pt Balabhu Umdekar popularly known as 'Kundalguru' of Gwalior gharana has the credit of composing and collecting many raagmalas. In his book 'Raag Sumanmala', many Raagmalas have been cited. One of the Raagmalas from 'Raag Sumanmala' has been given below with notation.

सुधर सहेली संग सखियन मिल,
गुन कलियन को हार लियो
दरसन की खटपट के जब बस,
देखत तब मन भई लाचारी,

Antara

प्रीत करन परदेसी प्रियसो,
काहे सुहागिन तु ललचाइ
जो बस रंग गौर सारंग के,
धनसिरी धन तुम सोच विचारी।

Sthayee : Tala Tritala

नि	नि	प	प	ग	–	म	–	म	म	नि	प	ध	ध	प	प
सु	ध	र	स	हे	ऽ	ली	ऽ	सं	ग	स	खि	य	न	मि	ल
X				3				X				2			
ध	ध	सां	रें	सां	सां	ध	निप	ग	प	ग	रे	सा	–	–	–
गु	न	क	लि	य	न	के	ऽऽ	हा	ऽ	र	लि	ये	ऽ	ऽ	ऽ
X				3				X				2			
ध	ध	सां	सां	नि	प	ग	म	प	ध	नि	ध	ग	म	रे	सा
द	र	रा	न	की	ऽ	ख	ट	प	ट	के	ऽ	ज	ब	ब	स
X				3				X				2			
ध	प	नि	नि	ध	ध	प	प	ग	म	ग	–	रे	ग	म	–
दे	ऽ	ख	त	त	ब	म	न	भ	ई	ला	ऽ	चा	ऽ	री	ऽ
X				3				X				2			

Antara

म	प	नि	नि	सां	सां	सां	सां	ध	–	प	–	प	नि	सां	–
प्री	ऽ	त	क	र	न	प	र	दे	ऽ	सी	ऽ	प्रि	य	सो	ऽ
X				3				X				2			
सं	–	नि	प	ग	–	प	म	ग	–	म	म	रे	–	सा	–
का	ऽ	हे	सु	हा	ऽ	ग	म	तू	ऽ	ल	ल	चा	ऽ	ई	ऽ
X				3				X				2			
ग	–	ग	ग	ग	–	म	ग	–	म	रे	ग	रे	म	ग	–
जो	ऽ	ब	स	रं	ऽ	ग	गो	ऽ	र	सा	ऽ	रं	ग	के	ऽ
X				3				X				2			
नि	सा	ग	म	प	प	ध	प	ग	–	प	प	ग	–	रे	सा
ध	न	रि	रि	ध	न	तु	म	सो	ऽ	च	बि	चा	ऽ	गे	ऽ
X				3				X				2			

The above Raagmala is composed in Rag Sughrai, Gunkali, Khat, Lachari Todi, Desi, Suha Gaud Sarang and Dhanashree.

Instrumentalists have also adopted the form of Raagmala. Late Ustad Bilayat Khan Saheb used to play Raagmala on his sitar. This researcher has also heard to Pt. Uma Shankar Mishra playing the Raagmala on sitar.

Raagmala form of singing also finds place in Vaishnav music. In Haveli Sangeet Raagmala is very much in vogue. Here is one example of Raagmala, which is sung in Haveli Sangeet tradition.

सारंग नयनी री काहे को कियौ एतोमान।
गौरी गहेरू छाड़ मिलि लालें मन क्रम वचन यादें होत कल्यान।।
जिन हित करे री तु नट नागर सों भैरों ही देवगान।।
मुरली तान कान्हरौ गावत सुन लैरी कान।
रंग रंगीली सुधर नायकी तु जिय में न अडान।।
नन्ददास केदारौ करिकें यो ही विहाय गयौ मान।।[19]

*देवगान stands for देवगान्धार, अडान for अडाना and विहाय for विहाग

The above composition of Shri Swami Nandadasa is an exquisite piece of Literature. At the same time it has great musical value. The music of Haveli tradition abounds in such compositions. The underlined names indicate the different ragas, which have been used in the composition.

In Islamic tradition a type of songs called 'Sokhwani' is sung during the Moharrum. Beautiful Raagmala compositions are found in these type of music. No instrument is used during the Moharrum being a mourning period. Here is an example:

एक रोज़ जनाबे हसन और हज़रते शब्बीर
नाना से बसद नाज़ करते थे तकरीर
हम दोनो हक गऐ चाहे कुरान के तफ़सीर
और आप को मनजूर बहत किसी की ये तोकीर
फरमाया के तुह्मारे लिये कुरानो दोनो
बलके मुभ्क नाना की तुम जान हो दोनो[20]

This composition is composed in Ragas Darbari, Malkauns, Hindol, Bageshwari, Lalit Pancham and Sohini.

Raagmala or Raagsagar is prevalent among the singers of different gharanas of Khayal. Late Ustad Mustaque Hussain Khan of Rampur Sahaswan gharana composed many Raagsagar. One characteristic of his Raagsagar is that it is sung without tala. Recently, this researcher has also heard to Pt. Gokulutsavjee Maharaj, singing his own composed Raagmala.

It is to be observed that in most of the Raagmalas the Ragas in which the various lines of the composition are to be sung, have been mentioned.

In the preceding chapter we have cited one composition by Tansen in which various Ragas have been mentioned. This practice is still followed.

In some Raagmala compositions, talas also vary along with change of Ragas.

Bamani Sargam or Svar Sagar

Imagination is the backbone of any creative art and music is no exception. Bamani Sargam or Svarsagar is the outcome of this essential element of art forms. Svara was one of the six angas of Prabandha. As such it has always been a part of closed forms. We have discussed a Prabandha called Svarartha, which conveyed the desired meaning through svaras or sargams. With the decline of Prabandhas gradually the svarartha type of compositions fell into disuse. However, after sometime it regained currency with the new name Bamani Sargam or Svarsagar.

Bamani is an Urdu/Persian word which means 'with meaning'. The meaning of the Sanskrit word Svarartha is svara =musical notes, Artha=meaning. Thus the word Bamani is synonymous with svarartha. In the present scenario of Hindustani music, this form is rarely heard. This researcher approached a number of musicians and musicologists, but could not collect more than a handful of compositions.

In some of the leading gharanas, a few Bamani Sargams are found. However, it has been observed that the musicians prefer to present vilmbit and drut khayals rather than Bamani Sargams. These compositions have been preserved as precious collections with representatives of various gharanas. Very rarely do we find Bamani sargams as a part of a full fledged recital.

An example of a Bamani Sargam, which is sung by some of the exponents of Gwalior gharana is given below with notation.

निर गगरी गिरी नार सें, सिर सिगरी गंगामग गिर परी।
पर धन मेरे सीस गगरी मोरे नारन मग गिर परी मोरी[21]

Raas Yaman, Teen Taal

ग	ग	रि	गि	रि	ना	ऽ	र	से	ऽ	ऽ	ऽ	ऽ	ऽ	सि	र
ग	ग	रे	ग	रे	नि़	ऽ	रे	सा	ऽ	ऽ	ऽ	ऽ	ऽ	स	रे
0				3				X				2			
स	ग	रि	गं	ऽ	गा	म	ग	गि	र	प	ऽ	ऽ	रि,	नि	र
सा	ग	रे	ग	ऽ	ग	म	ग	ग	रे	प	ऽ	ऽ	रे	नि़	रे
0				3				X				2			

Antara

प	र	ध	न	मे	ऽ	रे	ऽ	सी	ऽ	स	ग	ग	री	मो	रे
प	रे	ध	नि	म	ऽ	रे	ऽ	सां	ऽ	सां	गं	गं	रें	मं	रें
0				3				X				2			
ना	ऽ	र	न	म	ग	गि	र	प	ऽ	ऽ	रि	म	रि,	नि	र
नि	ऽ	रें	नि	म	ग	ग	रे	प	ऽ	ऽ	रे	म	रे,	नि	रे
0				3				X				2			

Late Pt Balabhau 'Kundalguru' of Gwalior Gharana has cited many compositions of this type in his book 'Raag Sumanmala'. One of the compositions given by him is a composition of 'Sadarang'.

Raag Bhoopali

सुधे पग परो सारे गोप गोपि पदपे गिरे सगरे रंग
सेारंग गिर परेसो।।
पगपे दस सीस सदा सरस पग रस सुंदर सदारंग दस
पदपे गीर गिरेसो।।

Teen Taal

सु	ऽ	ऽ	धे	ऽ	प	ऽ	ग	प	ऽ	ऽ	रा	ऽ	सा	ऽ	रे
सां	ऽ	ऽ	ध	ऽ	प	ऽ	ग	प	ऽ	ऽ	रे	ऽ	सा	ऽ	रे
0				3				X				2			
गे	ऽ	प	गो	ऽ	पि	प	द	पे	गी	ऽ	रे	स	ग	रें	ऽ
ग	ऽ	प	ग	ऽ	प	प	ध	प	ग	ऽ	रे	स	ग	रं	ऽ
0				3				X				2			
र	ग	ऽ	सो	ऽ	रं	ग	ऽ	गी	ऽ	र	प	ऽ	रे	सो	ऽ
रे	ग	ऽ	स	ऽ	रे	ग	ऽ	ग	ऽ	रे	प	ऽ	रे	सा	ऽ
0				3				X				2			

Antara

प	ग	पे	द	स	सी	ऽ	स	स	दा	ऽ	स	र	स	ऽ	प
प	ग	प	ध	सां	सां	ऽ	सां	सां	धा	ऽ	सां	रें	सां	ऽ	प
0				3				X				2			
ग	र	स	ऽ	सु	ऽ	दं	र	स	दा	ऽ	ऽ	रं	ग	ऽ	ऽ
गं	रें	सां	ऽ	सां	ऽ	ध	रें	सां	धा	ऽ	ऽ	रें	ग	ऽ	ऽ
0				3				X				2			
द	स	ऽ	ऽ	प	ऽ	ऽ	ऽ	द	पे	गी	ऽ	ऽ	रे	सो	
ध	सां	ऽ	ऽ	प	ऽ	ऽ	ऽ	ध	प	ग	ऽ	ऽ	रें	सा	[22]
0				3				X				2			

It is evident from the above composition that Bamani Sargam was very much in use during the time of Sadarang.

Although most of the composers of modern time have avoided this form of singing, still we have obtained some modern compositions. Here is an example of this type of composition which is composed by none other than the great Pt. Ravi Shankar.

Raag Yaman, Taal–Rupak

धन धन सुर सागर सरस्वती
में परूँ पग तोरे।
वीणा पाणी संगीत रानी
साधन मे करूँ तोरे।।[23]

This composition has been acquired from Dr. Suneera Kasliwal. According to Dr. Kasliwal this composition has been composed by Pt. Ravi Shankar for one orchestra in 1981 in Banaras. At that time Panditjee was a visiting Professor of Faculty of Performing Arts, Banaras Hindu University, Varanasi. The composition is a small, five to six minutes piece. It is in the praise of Ma Saraswati, the goddess of knowledge and composed in Rupak tala, i.e. 7 beats. Raga is Yaman. After a sitar piece of offbeat, the composition starts from the first matra.

Although a very simple piece, it throws light on the rare quality of the composer and his creativity. The composition was meant for the students that is why it is very simple but on the other hand it has aesthetical and formatical beauty which bears a clear stamp of its composer i.e. Pandit Ravi Shankar.

REFERENCES

1. Sargam, Tilana, Chaturang and Tappa, Article by Bimal Rai, SRA, Vol. 7, No. 1 August 1986, p. 11.
2. Agra Gharana Prampara Gayaki Aur Chhije, Ramanlal Mehta, p. 66.
3. Kramik Pustak Malika, Part-III, p. 667.
4. Kramik Pustak Malika, Part-III, p. 271.
5. Raag Vigyan, Part-III, p. 60.
6. Sumati Mutatkar, 'Geet Nirjhari', Kanishka Publishers, 2002, p. 113.
7. Acquired from Pt. R.C. Bhatt.

8. Acquired from Mukul Shivputra.
9. Raag Vigyan, Part II, p. 111.
10. Raga Kalpadrum, Part-II, p. 30.
11. Raag Vigyan, Part II, p. 173.
12. Kramik Pustak Malika, Part-III, p. 84.
13. Raga Vigyan, Part-I, p. 49.
14. Agra Gharana Gayaki Aur Chhije, Ramanlal Mehta, pp. 14-15.
15. Pushtimrgiya Mandiron ki Sangeet Parampara, Dr. Satyabhan Sharma, p. 194.
16. Acquired from Pt. R.C. Bhatt.
17. Raag Sumanmala by Balabhow 'Kundalguru', p. 127.
18. Bhav Rang Lahiri by Pt Balvant Rai Bhatt, p. 184.
19. Pushtimargiya Mandiron ki Sangeet Parampara, Dr. Satyabhan Sharma, p. 183.
20. Acquired from Ustad Iqbal Ahmed Khan.
21. Acquired from a Mukul Shivputra.
22. Raag Sumanmala, p. 154.
23. Acquired from Dr. Suneera Kasliwal.

Chapter–4

Prospects and Problems of Preservation

It is often mistakenly believed that cultural values and symbols are most distinctly and justifiably preserved in the popular and established forms of Art, Music, Dance etc. On the contrary, the lesser known forms of cultural expressions are also very much, the vehicles of culture and all that it stands for. This is particularly true in the tradition of Hindustani classical music, where the lesser known forms have silently done what their better known counterparts like Dhrupad and Khayal had been doing.

It was rather natural that the lesser known forms were eclipsed by the emergence of Dhrupad and Khayal. But their revival and preservation is significant in two contexts. First, it brings back the earlier flag bearers of Hindustani music into the rightful place they deserve. Second, their presence in the domain of Hindustani music adds variety and charm to even the existing forms.

Oral tradition is the backbone of Hindustani classical music. It has been systematized in different styles and streams leading to the formation of different houses of music—"The Gharanas". Gharanas are the abodes of compositions hundreds of years old. Indeed those delicate variations and manoeuvres in the compositions which are at the heart and soul of higher echelons of Hindustani classical music would have been lost in the wilderness of print but for these Gharanas. Compositions more than hundreds of years old are still performed and preserved due to the existence of the Gharana system. The musicians representing different Gharanas undertake two responsibilities. One being their duty and the other being their ability. First they carry on the legacy of their own Gharanas and dutifully pay obeisance to the form which their Gharana's founding fathers set and established. Secondly over a period of pains taking effort and endeavour, they keep on adding the tinges and flavour of their own individual style to the existing forms of their Gharanas. This is how Hindustani classical music maintains its purity all the while adapting to the times. So, the capable musicians of different Gharanas have the responsibility to revive the lesser known forms. These days the Gurus and the disciples are pressed for time. Gone are the days when the disciple spent as much time as possible with the Guru. While the musical tradition of yore was about learning a variety of compositions from renditions by Guru, today the aspect of mastery of a wide spectrum of compositions is no more considered wise and necessary. The disciples are satisfied with obtaining a couple or two of Khayals in a Raga and then take flight solely on their feeble wings of learning, albeit with no excellence, into the realm of Hindustani music. The old system can be revived by teaching some lesser known compositions. This process not only enhances knowledge and stock of the students but will also go a long way in the preservation of these compositions for the posterity. The Gurus with their vast knowledge of compositions can themselves compose Chaturang, Trivat etc. In the process the students would also learn a variety of compositions.

While Gharanas are the interface between learned and learners of music, concerts are the interface between the learned and the interested of music. It is the venue of exchange of entertainment by the audience for satisfaction and sense of fulfillment of the artistes. It has become customary today to present a small piece at the end of a concert. For instance a Khayal singer would wind up his performance with Thumri and Dadra. This indeed is to exhibit the performers command over a wide variety of forms.

For the last few decades Bhajan has replaced this practice in a big way. Many eminent musicians present devotional pieces as their ending item. They can make it a practice to do sing a Chaturang, Trivat or Bamani Sargam too. Soon, the listeners would also get interested. We may cite an example. For the last two years we have been hearing Ragamala compositions as an ending piece quite often. In the year 2004, All India Radio concert featured two artistes, one each in vocal and instrumental, who presented Raagmala compositions.

All India Radio has played a significant role in the propagation of Indian Classical music. In fact it was Dr. B.V. Keskar – the then information and broadcasting minister who was instrumental in allotting sizable slots for classical items in AIR. This tradition is still being followed with some modifications. The All India Radio broadcasts classical music items at different times. For example a schedule of classical items, which All India Radio, Delhi broadcasts is given below:

7:30 a.m. to 7:45 a.m. at Delhi B

8:15 a.m. to 8:45 a.m. at Delhi A

11:30 a.m. to 12:00 p.m. at Delhi A

4:30 p.m. to 5:00 p.m. at Delhi B

8:20 p.m. to 8:45 p.m. at Delhi B

9:00 p.m. to 9:15 p.m. at Delhi A

10:30 p.m. to 11:00 p.m. at Delhi A (Thursday)

Monday 10:00 p.m. to 11:00 p.m. Delhi A

Tuesday 10:00 p.m. to 11:00 p.m. Chayan Delhi A

Friday (Alternate) 10:00 p.m. to 11:00 p.m. Mehfil Delhi A

Besides these slots, a national programme is held every Saturday from 10 p.m. to 11 p.m. Another national programme under the title 'Sunday night concerts' is held every Sunday at 10 p.m. to 11 p.m. All India Radio also conducts Akashvani Sangeet Sammelans every year.

Considering the place of lesser known forms in Hindustani music it is desirable that All India Radio introduce regular programmes for the same. To begin with, morning slots with 15 minutes duration preferably between 9 and 9.15 a.m. could be used to broadcast programmes (twice a month or so) on lesser known forms. Later the duration or frequency could be gradually increased and the broadcast could be shifted to prime time.

All India Radio preserve recordings of great maestros of Classical music in their Music Archives. The lesser known forms could also be added to these Archives through recordings of compositions sung by eminent musicians. AIR as a mass medium have considerable role in propagating music. AIR also generate and influence public taste. An integral part of the process of preservation is implanting the subject matter in public consciousness. This fundamental applies well to the preservation of music. And AIR taking initiative in propagating lesser known forms through bimonthly or more frequent programmes would be a right step in the preservation of these forms which are disappearing from mainstream Hindustani Music.

Musicians can do yeomen service to the preservation of other lesser known forms if they adapt them for their performances. They can first begin presenting the forms in between their main and ending pieces as a specimen of a rare composition i.e. after ending the Khayal a Trivat, Chaturang or some such form can be presented. Finally the artiste may wind up with a Thumri or a Bhajan as the case may be. Performers are the ones who change public taste. Certainly it would be a change for the better.

The Dhrupad singers could also adopt the Trivat form of singing as an ending piece in a Dhurpad concert. As Pakhawaj is the main accompanying instrument of Dhrupad and the Trivat is also composed of the bols of Pakhawaj, so it would be easier for a Dhrupad singer to adopt the style of Trivat singing. In this regard, the Dhrupadiyas can give new dimensions to the style of presentation of Trivat.

A perceptible and obvious reason for certain forms having become lesser known was due to its disappearance from Public domain of music (apart from the conspicuous absence from the musicians' and musicologists' own interest span). The remedy to this misfortune is to bring them back into the public sphere. Translation of these forms into notation and publishing them in a book form would achieve the aforesaid goal. For understanding the subtle nuances CD/Cassette could also be provided with the book.

A distinguished musician and musicologist to whom the highest credit goes for rescuing Indian classical music from decadence, decline and extinction is Late Pandit Vishnu Narayan Bhatkhande. At a great personal sacrifice and suffering, and inspired by only one aim, Bhatkhande throughout his life undertook the herculean task of reviving Indian Classical music. It may be mentioned that hundreds of compositions have survived today because of Pt. V.N. Bhatkhande.

In the last few decades of the nineteenth century Bhatkhande found that the Indian Classical music, although it had a glorious history, had reached the bottom of degeneration and was looked down upon as unworthy, superfluous and vulgar—a subject fit for loafers and vagabonds. Bhatkhande radically altered the scene and put music once again on its high pedestal. Vishnu Narayan Bhatkhande wàs a unique personality endowed with scholarship, creativity, poetic sensibilities, capacity for patient and hard work and devotion for the Indian musical tradition and above all humility. Bhatkhande began his work with collection of hundreds of compositions from different Gharanas. He analysed them and formulated the theory of Indian Music underlying these compositions. He also formulated an easy and expressive notation system for Hindustani Music and introduced a new method of collective education in music and wrote textbooks and gave music the form and shape of an academic subject. Due to the lack of notation, the compositions of the great composers like Tansen, Bakoo, Baiju, Surdas etc could not survive. Although in some books like Sahasras, Kitab-e-Navras, the verbal texts of the great composers are available, still these are not enough to revive these compositions.

The most important person among Bhatkhande's contemporaries was Vishnu Digambar Paluskar who was a noted musician and a musicologist who launched a similar movement to that of Bhatkhande's.

Though both Bhatkhande and Paluskar were contemporaries, the work that each undertook, in the field of music, was rather different in nature. Whereas Bhatkhande dedicated his whole life to research in ancient and contemporary Indian music and endeavoured to give a systematic shape to it, Paluskar laboured to spread music practically and to gain for it a respectable place in society. As has been stated earlier, till that time the musicians were considered as belonging to the lower strata of society and respectable persons shunned them though they appreciated their art. The modern generation would perhaps find it difficult to comprehend the plight of the Indian musicians and the art of music in those days. These two stalwarts worked for the uplift of music and their emancipation of music propagators with undaunted courage and tenacity. V.D. Paluskar himself was a great composer and composed many Chaturgas and Trivats and hence contributed towards the revival of the lesser known forms. Following the footsteps of the stalwarts like V. N. Bhatkhande and V.D. Paluskar, the present generation can collect and publish lesser known forms of Hindustani Classical Music. With a little effort this goal can be achieved.

Music is an integral part of culture and it is the medium through which cultural symbols are transported across generations and time periods. It is also the phenomenon which translates ideas into realities. Music is thus a necessary input to the growth of societies and equally to the growing in the societies. The young minds are fertile grounds for learning. Mere academics create opaqueness to the culture of the society since it singularly imparts knowledge dimensions of culture, grossly ignoring the aesthetic aspects of culture.

Indeed realizing the value of music in culture, it has been judiciously introduced in educational institutions as part of curriculum. Music today is taught in schools, colleges and universities as a full-fledged subject of study. But the emphasis is given to Khayal and Dhrupad forms. This, it is acknowledged, is in keeping with the spirits of popularity and appeal. Some of the lesser known forms have also been partly introduced into curriculum, but only as theoretical studies. The practical learning is not at all insisted. But study of music bereft of its practice is meaningless and remains at the level of an awareness and not study.

Let us look into some of the portions of the curriculum of B.A. (Hon) Music, 3rd year of Delhi University.

Paper V Ancient and Medieval History upto Sharangdeva

Vedic Age: Sama and Rik, Stobhaksharas the notes of Vedic music, gramageya gana aranyageya gana, Poorvarchika, Uttararchika Udatt, anudatta, swarita, Vedic and loukik scales, Vedic instruments, verities of Samans for various phenomena or nature, Panchavidha Sama, Musical references in Pratishakyas, Ramayana, Mahabharata and Puran.

General review of the following authors: Bharata, Matanga, Someshwar, Narad, Sharangdeva.

Paper VI History of Indian Music from the post Sharangadeva period to Modern times.

General review of the following authors: Ramamatya, Somanatha, Pundarika Vithala, Ahobala, Srinivasa, Venkatamakhin, Hridayanarain Deva, Lochana, Bhava Bhatta, Faqir Ullah, Mohammad Raza (Naghmate Asafi) Hakim Mohd, Karam Imam, Pratap Singh (Radha Govind Sangit Sara), F. Clements, Fox Strangways, S.M. Tagore, K.D. Banerjee, Bhatkhande, also relevant information from Ain-i-Akbari.

Paper VII Musicology—Theory of Indian Music (Applied)

Present forms of music in notation and their ways of rendering on voice and instruments based on practical. Alapa, Dhrupads,

Hori, Khayal, Tappa, Thumri, Tarana, Chaturang, Swarmatika, Raga Malika and Raagmala. Vilambit and drut, Masitkhani and Rajakhani gats, combination of different ragas. Different schools regarding techniques (Gharanas), vocal and instrumental (Stringed and percussion). Detailed study of the ragas prescribed in I, II and III year. Basic knowledge of the compositional forms of Karnatak music, viz. Kriti, Pallavi, Tillana, Varnam, Padama Javeli.

Paper VIII Practical III Performance Test (Vocal and Instrumental)

Performance of half an hour, planned by the candidate within the prescribed Ragas:

1. Pooriya Dhanshri, 2. Todi, 3. Kamod, 4. Multani, 5. Gaud Sarang, 6. Kedar, 7. Patdeep, 8. Jaijaiwanti, 9. Chhayanat, 10. Malkauns.

Paper IX Practical IV (Vocal and Instrumental)

Ragalap in all the prescribed Ragas of Paper VIII Dhrupad or Dhamar or Sadra Compositions in each of the Ragas. Dhrupad with Layakari and Upaj in any one Raga, Dhamar with Layakari and Upaj in any other Raga. Gat with elaboration in any three of the following talas: Dhamar, Ektaal, Chautal, Jhaptal, Adachautal.

Paper X Practical (Vocal and Instrumental)

Viva Voce—Vilambit Khayal with gayaki and Madhyalaya Khayal with gayaki in each of the prescribed Ragas of Paper VIII. Masitkhani and Razakhani gats with elaboration in all the prescribed Ragas.

We have seen in the practical course, the forms Dhrupad, Khayal, Dhamar and Sadra have been introduced. Along with these forms, the other lesser known forms like Chaturang, Trivat, Raagmala, Bamani—Sargam etc., should have been introduced so as to make these forms popular at least among the students of music.

The lesser known forms, like Chaturang and Ragamalika have been included as a part of theoretical study. The other forms like Trivat and Bamani - Sargam should be introduced in the curriculum so that students would come to know about varieties of compositional forms. Also in the post-graduation level, these lesser known forms should find place both for theoretical and practical study. In this regard credit goes to Banaras Hindu University. In the music department of B.H.U. forms like Chaturang and Trivat are taught in the graduation level. The University should take steps to introduce other forms also.

Different musicological societies and institutions also have some responsibilities in reviving the lesser known forms. They should conduct seminars and workshops on the lesser known forms so that valuable opinions of eminent scholars could be obtained. Different government and non-government institutions and societies have contributed a lot in propagating Hindustani classical music. Societies like Indian Musicological Society of Baroda, Music Academy of Madras, Sangeet Research Academy of Kolkata and National Centre for Performing Arts etc. have contributed a lot in reviving Indian classical music. In this regard credit should be given to Sangeet Research Academy of Kolkata. Sangeet Research Academy held one seminar on lesser known forms in 1986 and had invited eminent scholars like late Thakur Jaidev Singh, Vidushi Sumati Mutatkar etc. SRA had also published the annual journal in 1986 August from which much information could be obtained regarding some of the lesser known forms. In this seminar forms like Chaturang, Trivat, Tarana, Sargam etc. were discussed, while forms like Bamani Sargam and Raagmala were left out.

The keynote address of the seminar was given by Late Thakur Jaidev Singh. Thakur Jaidev Singh had elaborately discussed different rare compositional forms. Chaturang and Trivat also found place in his address. According to Thakur Jaidev Singh, the word Trivat was evolved from the Sanskrit word 'Trivart'. He stated that Trivat consisted of three elements, viz—Pada, sargam and bols of tarana. The Patas of Pakhawaj was not there. He also gave example of this type of Trivat in Raga Kalingada. He also threw light on other forms of Hindustani Classical music like tappa, tarana, lakshangeet, sargam geet etc.

The article written by Vidushi Sumati Mutatkar is of great substance. According to her the forms Chaturang, Trivat, Tarana etc., are the outcome of the Karana Prabandhas. She also elaborately discussed the historical aspects of Tarana form of singing.

Besides these two scholars, other personalities like Sri Bimal Rai, Prof. Vidyadhar Vyas etc., also contributed to the Journal with their valuable writings.

The history of Chaturang, Trivat, Raag Mala and Bamani Sargams is the tale of transition of the well known forms of Hindustani Classical music of yesteryears into the lesser known forms of today. Their journey into unknown is not too distant. The gradual disappearance of the lesser known forms could be halted only through purposeful interventions by all stakeholders, namely Gharanas, musicians, musicologists, students and the general public. The measures for preservation discussed above are few of the efforts to preserve lesser known forms. A serious deliberation and initiation of actions to preserve these forms are the demands of the day.

Chapter–5

Compositions with Notations Collected from Different Authoritative Books and Musicians

In chapter three a detailed description of the lesser known forms has been carried out analytically. For this purpose verbal texts of some compositions have been given. In this chapter their notations, along with, some more compositions, are being presented. The purpose of this chapter is to highlight musical elements of these forms thereby to prove that such compositions are in no way inferior to their better known counterparts. Let us begin with the well known Chaturang in the Raga Des "Chaturanga ko Gave".

CHATURANG

Rag Des–Tritala (Madhyalaya)

								Sthayee							
														[म]ग	म
														च	त
ग	रे	ग	[ग]सा	–	रे	म	प	[सां]निसां	रे	सां	नि̱	धप	ध	[प]म	म
रं	ग	को	गा	ऽ	वे	र	स	रौंऽ	ऽ	ग	त	सोंऽ	ऽ	क	र
x				3				x				2			
[म]ग	–	ग	ग	ग	म	रे	ग	गम	पप	म	ग	रे	ग	नि़	सा
ती	ऽ	व	र	को	ऽ	म	ल	देऽ	ऽऽ	ख	भा	ऽ	ल	क	र
x				3				x				2			
रेग	सारे	म	–	प	प	[सां]नि	नि	[सां]नि	–	सां	नि	सां	नि	सां	–

(Contd.)

तऽ रऽ ती ऽ	व र अ ति	को ऽ म ल	सु र सों ऽ
x	3	x	2

सांनिसां रेंगं रें सां	नि सां नि सां	सांनिसां रें सां नि	धप ध पग म
न्या ऽऽ रो न्या	ऽ रो सु र	संऽ ऽ ग त	सोंऽऽ ऽ च त।
x	3	x	2

Antara

पम म म प	सांनि नि नि नि	सां सां – सांनि	– सां सां सां
दिर दिर दिर ता	ना ना दिर दिर	ता नो ऽ म्ता	ऽ न्ना दिर दिर
x	3	x	2

रें गं रें सां	रें नि सां सां	सां रें सां नि	धप ध धग म
तुं दिर दिर दिर	दिर दिर दिर दिर	दिर दिर दिर दा	ऽऽ नि, च त
x	3	x	2

Sanchari or Abhog

गम मनि – ध	– ध निध –	सांनि नि – ध	नि ध नि सां
उ नं ऽ चा	ऽ स को ऽ	ट ता ऽ न	ति न के ऽ
0	3	x	2

सां सारे सां नि	धप ध प –	मरे म प ध	(म) – मरे –
क ठीऽ न रे	गीऽ ऽ ले ऽ	हे ऽ ऽ ऽ	ब्यो ऽ रे ऽ
0	3	x	2

म म प प	सांनि नि सां –	निसां रें सां नि	ध प म ऽ
0	3	x	2

म मम मम पप	निनि निनि नि सां	ध नि सां –सां	नि सां रेंरें रेंरें
धा किट तक धुम	किट तक धि त्ता	ऽक् धि त्ता ऽक्	धि त्ता किड नग
0	3	x	2

निनि निनि सांसां सांसां	निसा निसारें सांसां निनि	ध प ध म	ग रे मग म
नग धिरि किट तक	तक धीऽऽकिड नग	त घ्डा ऽन् तक्	धा ऽ, च त।
0	3	x	2

The third or the last part has been termed as Sanchari or Abhog. But if we analyse its musical contents, it would be clear that it is in the nature of Abhog. Sanchari part dwells on the Madhya and Mandra Saptaks whereas the above part is in the Madhya and Tar Saptak.

CHATURANG

Raga–Jaunpuri–Tritala

Sthayee

प नि ध प	[प]ध म पप मप	[म]ग – [सा]रे म	प – – –
च त रं ग	र स सऽ नऽ	गा ऽ ऽ ई	ये ऽ ऽ ऽ
0	3	X	2
[नि]ध – – [नि]ध	– प पध मप	[म]ग – रे [सा]रे	– रे सा सा
ले ऽ ऽ जा	ऽ नि येऽ ऽऽ	सू ऽ र ता	ऽ ल प र
0	3	X	2
[नि]सा सा गं गं	रें रें सां सां	[सां]नि – सां रें	[नि]ध – प धम
म्रा ला ऽ प	क र के सु	ना ऽ ऽ इ	ये ऽ ऽ ऽऽ
0	3	X	2
मप पसां [नि]ध प			
चऽ तऽ रं ग			
0			

Antara

म म प प	[नि]ध – [सां]नि नि	सां – सां –	[सां]नि सां सां सां
न द्रे धि ति	ला ऽ ना त	दीं ऽ दीं ऽ	त न न न
X	2	0	3
[नि]ध [नि]ध – ध	सां सां – रें	[म]गं – – –	रें – ध प
नि ता ऽ रे	नि ता ऽ रे	ता ऽ ऽ ऽ	दीं ऽ म्दी ऽम्
X	2	0	3
सा ऽ सा ऽ	सा रे म ऽ	रे म प ऽ	म प ध ऽ
X	2	0	3

								(प)म	–	–	प	(नि)ध	–	–	नि
प	ध	नि	ऽ	ध	नि	सां	ऽ	हा	ऽ	ऽ	र्ष	वे	ऽ	ऽ	गु
x				2				0				3			
सां	–	–	सां	(सां)नि	सां	सां	–	(नि)ध	–	–	ध	सां	–	सां	रें
यौ	ऽ	ऽ	कि	फ	ऽ	र्दा	ऽ	त	ऽ	ऽ	र्क	नू	ऽ	स	ऽ
x				2				0				3			
सां	रें	गं	रें	(नि)ध	–	प	–	(म)प	गं	–	गं	रें	नि	म	म
ता	ऽ	ऽ	कि	नौं	ऽ	ऽ	ऽ	बा	ऽ	ऽ	ज	चु	ऽ	फ	र
x				2				0				3			
पध	निसां	–	नि	सां	–	–	सां	(म)गं	–	–	(सा)रें	–	(सा)रें	सां	–
दोऽ	ऽऽ	ऽ	सु	फ	ऽ	ऽ	र	यू	ऽ	ऽ	रो	ऽ	ज	रा	ऽ
x				2				0				3			
नि	सां	निसां	रें	ध	–	प	–	प	सां	ध	ध				
दु	नि	यांऽ	कु	नौं	ऽ	ऽ	ऽ	च	त	रं	ग				
x				2				0							

In the above composition the main phrases of the Raga Jaunpuri are clearly visible e.g. प नि धप, ध म प ध म प, ग – रे म प—the opening line; the beginning of the Antara म म प प ध ध नि नि सां : पगं रें or संग रे etc., etc.

CHATURANG
Raga Yaman—Teen Taal

संगीत मत करत ग्यान ध्यान
सप्त सुरन संपुरन चतरंग
मंग मंप निधनि सांरंसां गंगरेंसं
निध नि प ध मं प गमगरे गमपमं
ना दिर दिर तनन तुं दिर दिर तनन
तोंमतन ननन दीम्तन नननन

तिर किट ता धुमकिट ता, तिरकिट ता धुमकिट ता,
तिरकिट ता धुमकिट ता।।[1]

नि	धनिध(प)	–		प	–	ग	प	(प)	–	–	प	ग	–	–	रे
सं	ऽऽऽ	गी	ऽ	त	ऽ	ऽ	म	त	ऽ	ऽ	क	र	ऽ	ऽ	त
x				2				0				3			
ग	मंमं	गरे	गरे	सा	सासा	ऩिध़	ऩिध़	सा	गरे	गम	गरे	सारे	सा	सा	–
ग्या	ऽऽ	ऽऽ	ऽन	घ्या	ऽऽ	ऽऽ	ऽन	स	ऽऽ	प्ता	सुऽ	रऽ	न	सं	ऽ
x				2				0				3			
सा	रे	[स]रे	ग	[रे]ग	मं	[ग]मं	प	[प]नि	[ध]निध	प	प	ग	रे	सा	सा
पु	ऽ	ऽ	ऽ	ऽ	ऽ	ऽ	ऽ	ऽ	ऽऽ	र	न	च	त	रे	ग
x				2				0				3			
मं	ग	मं	प	–	नि	ध	नि	सां	–	रे	सां	गं	गं	रे	सां
x				2				0				3			
नि	ध	नि	प	ध	मं	प	–	ग	म	ग	रे	ग	मं	प	मं
x				2				0				3			
प	गग	पप	प	नि	ध	नि	सांसां	सांसां	सां	सां	सां	सां	–	रें	गं
ना	दिर	दिर	त	न	न	तुं	दिर	दिर	त	न	न	तो	ऽ	मम	न
x				2				0				3			
ग	रें	सां	सां	सां	रें	सां	नि	ध	प	ग	रे	गंगं- गंगं	गं-	रेंरें- रेंरें	रें-
न	न	न	न	दी	ऽ	म्त	न	न	न	न	न	तिर- किट	तऽ	धुम- किट	ताऽ
x				2				0				3			

निनिनिनि	नि–	पपपप	प–	गमगग	रेऽ	सासासासा	सा–	[प]नि	[ध]नि	(प)	–	प	–
तिरकिट	ताऽ	धुमकिट	ताऽ	तिरकिट	ताऽ	धुमकिट	ताऽ	सं	ऽ	गी	ऽ	त	ऽ
x				2				0				3	

Chaturang of Agra Gharana
Raag Marwa–Teen Tala

Sthayee

चतरंग सब मील गाइये, गाइये बजाइये आरै रीझाइये

Antara

मोहम्मदश वरकाज सोहाग नाचत सब मिल दे दे तारी
सा ग मं ग रे सा छोम्छननन छोम्छननन,
तक धी तक धी तक तिरकिट तक धी कड़ां धा धा

Sthayee

ध	मं	ध	मं	ग	मं	ध	मं	ग	रे	–	मं	ग	रे	सा	–
च	त	रे	ग	स	व	मी	ल	गा	ऽ	ऽ	इ	ये	ऽ	ऽ	ऽ
0				3				X				2			

नि	रे	ग	मं	ग	रे	सा	–	मं	ध	मं	ध	म	ग	रे	सा
गां	इ	ये	ब	जा	इ	ये	ऽ	ओ	ऽ	र	री	झा	इ	ये	ऽ
0				3				X				2			

Antara

ग	ग	ग	ग	मं	–	ध	ध	सां	–	सा	सां	सांनि	रें	सां	सां
मो	ह	म्म	द	शा	ऽ	व	र	का	ऽ	ज	सो	हाऽ	ऽ	ऽ	ग
X				2				0				3			

नि	रें	नि	ध	नि	ध	म	ग	रें	ग	ग	मं	ग	रें	सा	ऽ
ना	ऽ	–च	त	स	ब	मि	ल	दे	ऽ	ऽ	दे	ता	ऽ	री	ऽ
X				2				0				3			

सा	गा	ऽ	मं	ग	रें	सा	–	नि	ऽ	रें	नि	ध	मं	ग	रें
सा	गा	ऽ	मं	ग	रें	सा	ऽ	छो	ऽ	ऽ	म्छ	न	न	न	न
X				2				0				3			

(Contd.)

सा	गा	ऽ	मं	ग	रें	सा	सा	सा	ग	ग	ग	मं	ध	ध	सां
छो	ऽ	ऽ	म्छ	न	न	न	न	तक	धीऽ	तक	धीऽ	तक	तिर	किट	तक
x				2				0				3			
नि	नि	रें	नि	ध	मं	ग	रें								
धी	कड़ा	ऽ	धा	धा	नि	धा	धा								

शुद सारंग (चतुरंग)

Sthayee

गाइये, सजना गुनिजन, बीच, ताल सुर, तान, वानि
उन जाने सकल विध ताहि भेद समझाय।

Antara

तनन दीऽम तारे तनन तन, देरेना, मंप निसां पनि
सरें मरें सांनि धप, मंप, रेम रेरें सांनि धाप
संनि धाप मंप रेम रेसा कृधान धान्धुम किट तक
धिन्ता धा धान धा धान धा रामरंग चतुरंग गीत सुनाये

															सा
															गा
नि	ध	पमं	प	म	रे	सानि़	सा	मरे	–	मं	मं	प	मं	प	सा
ऽ	इ	ये	ऽ	स	ज	ना	गु	नी	ऽ	य	न	बी	ऽ	च,	ता
रे	सा	नि	प़	सा	–	सा	मरे	म	रे	मं	प	धनि	सां	नि	रें
ऽ	ल	सु	र	ता	ऽ	न	बा	ऽ	नि	उ	न	नाऽ	ऽ	ने	स
सां	निध	मं	प	निसा	रें	सां	मंप	ध	प	नि	सा	रेमं	पध	प,	गा
क	लऽ,	बि	ध	ताऽ	ऽ	हि	भेऽ	ऽ	द	स	म	झाऽ	ऽऽ	य,	गा
3				x				2				0			

Antara

म	रे	मं	प	सां	–	सां	प	नि	सां	रें	सां	नि	ध	प	मंप
न	म	दी	ऽम	ता	ऽ	रे	त	न	न	त	न	दे	रे	ना,	मंप
निसां	पनि	सारें	मेरें	सांनि	धप	मंप	रेम	रेंरें	सांनि	धप	सांनि	धप	मंप	रेम	रेसा
मम	मम	रे	मंमं	पप	धध	मं	प	सांनि	रेसां	–प	मंध	प	–सा	नि़रे	सा
नुधा	ऽन	धा	धुम	किट	तक	धि	ता	धाऽ	नधा	ऽधा	ऽन	धा	ऽधा	ऽन	धा
नि़	सा	मम	रेसा	रे	मं	धध	पमं	प	नि	रेंरें	सांनि	प	मंध	प,	सां
रा	म	रंऽ	गऽ	च	तु	रंऽ	गऽ	गी	ऽ	तऽ	सुऽ	ना	ऽ	य	गा
3				X				2				0			

This Chaturang is a composition of Pt. Ramashray Jha (Ramrang). This composition is rich in literature as well as in musical parts. The Raga Suddha Sarang has been manifested very beautifully. This is evident that modern time composers are very much aware of the Chaturang form of singing.

यमन-चतुरंग

Sthayee

चतुरंग को कोउ भेद न पावे,
सेवा कर जो गुनी जनन की
कर विचार मन लावे

Antara

दिर दिर दा दा दिरदिर दानी
तनूऽम्त दारे दानी,
तनूऽतू ऽम्तनन
नि़ रे ग मं प ध नि सं रें सं न ध प मं ग मं
(तिट कत गदि गिन धा)
तिट कत गदि गिन धा
तिट कत गदि गिन
धा धीं धी धा धा धीं धीं धा[2]

Sthayee

स	सं	नि	ध	प	मं	प	मं	प	–	ग	रे	ऩि	रे	स	–
च	तु	रें	ग	को	ऽ	को	ऽ	भे	ऽ	द	न	पा	ऽ	वे	ऽ
0				3				x				2			

ऩि	–	रे	–	ग	–	मं	–	प	–	–	प	मं	ध	प	–
से	ऽ	वा	ऽ	क	र	जो	ऽ	गु	नी	ऽ	ज	न	न	की	ऽ
0				3				x				2			

मं	ध	नि	ध	प	मं	ग	रे	ऩि	रे	ग	रे	ऩि	रे	स	–
क	र	वि	चा	ऽ	र	म	न	ला	ऽ	ऽ	ऽ	ऽ	ऽ	वे	ऽ
0				3				x				2			

Although this is a very simple composition, the note combinations of Raga Yaman have been presented beautifully. This Chaturang will be beneficial for the beginner students of music.

Antara

मं	मं–	ग	ग	मं	गं	ध	–	सं	–	–	–	नि	रें	सं	–
दिर	दिर	दा	दा	दिर	दिर	दा	नी	त	तू	ऽ	म्त	दा	रे	दा	नी
0				3				x				2			

नि	रें	गं	रें	सं	नि	ध	प								
त	नू	ऽम्	तू	ऽम्	त	न	न	ऩि	रे	ग	मं	प	ध	नि	सं
0				3				x				2			

रें	सं	नि	ध	प	म	ग	मं	नि	रे	ग	मं	प	–	रे	ग
								तिट	कत	गदि	गिन	धा	ऽ	तिट	कत
0				3				x				2			

मं	ध	नि	–	ग	मं	ध	नि	सं	नि	ध	प	मं	ग	रे	स
गदि	गिन	धा	ऽ	तिट	कत	गदि	गिन	धा	धीं	धीं	धा	धा	धीं	धीं	धा
0				3				x				2			

CHATURANG

Raga Paraj – Teen Taal

Sthayee

						प	सां	नि	ध	प	ध	मं	ऽ	प	ध
						-च	तु	रं	ग	को	व	ना	-	ये	ऽ
				2				0				3			
सां	नि	ध	प	म	ग	ऽ	ऽ	सा	सा	ग	ग	मं	ध	मं	ध
सु	ध	म	त	सों	-	-	-	स	म्पु	र	न	रा	ग	गु	नी
X				2				0				3			
ध	सां	नि	मं	-	ध										
ती	व	र	गा	ऽ	ये										
X				2				0				3			

Antara

								ग	म	ग	म	प	ध	मं	प
								0				3			
ध	नि	ध	नि	सां	रें	नि	सा	रें	गं	रें	गं	रें	सां	नि	सां
X				2				0				3			
								सा	ऽ	ऽ	गऽ	ऽ	ऽ	मं	ऽ
ध	नि	सां	रें	सा	नि	ध	प	धा-	किट	तक	धुम	किट	तक	धुम	किट
X				2				0				3			
ऽ	ध	ऽ	ऽ	सां	ऽ	ऽ	ऽ	गंऽ	रेंऽ	सां	ऽ	निऽ	धऽ	प	ऽ
तक	धुम	किट	तक	धुम	किट	तक	तृक	धाऽ	किट	धा	धुम	किट	तक	धा	-
X				2				0				3			
सां	नि	ध	प	म	ग	प	सां								
क्डां	धा	क्डां	धा	क्डां	धा	च	तु								
X				2											

The above Chaturang is composed in Raga Paraj. The note combinations which are used in this Chaturang is different from today's Paraj. According to Ustad Iqbal Ahmad Khan, Raga Paraj of this kind is the original one. Although both the madhyams are used in this composition, the way of their use is different from today's Paraj.

Trivat in Raga Kedar
Teen Taal

Sthayee

तिरकिट तक धे धेन्ना धगीनधा धाधातुना।
धगीनधा धाधातुना धगीनधा धाधातुना।।

Antara

धा किटतक धुम किटतक धित्ता धा।
शुकरंग क्डां क्डां धाधाधा
क्डां क्डां धाधाधा
क्डां क्डां धाधाधा[3]

Sthayee

गम	धध	पप	ग	म	रे	सा	–	सा	रे	सा	मा	म	म	म	म
तिर	किट	तक	धे	ऽ	धे	न्ना	ऽ	ध	गी	न	धा	धा	धा	तू	ना
0				3				X				2			
ग	म	ग	म॑	प	प	प	प	म	नि॒	ध	प	म	म	म	म
ध	गी	न	धा	धा	धा	तु	ना	ध	गी	न	धा	धा	धा	तू	ना
0				3				X				2			

Antara

म	म्म	म्म	पप	पप	पप	नि	सां	रें	–	सां	नि	ध	प	म॑	प
धा	किट	त्क	धुम	किट	त्क	धि	त्त	धा	ऽ	ऽ	ऽ	शु	क	रं	ग
X				2				0				3			

(Contd.)

मं	–	मं	–	रें	रें	सां	–	प	–	रें	–	सां	नि	सां	–
क्डां	ऽ	क्डां	ऽ	धा	धा	धा	ऽ	क्डां	ऽ	क्डां	ऽ	धा	धा	धा	ऽ
x				2				0				3			
मं	प	सां	नि	ध	प	म	–								
क्डां	ऽ	क्डां	ऽ	धा	धा	धा	ऽ								
x				2											

TRIVAT

Raga Adana–Teen Taal

Sthayee

										ऽ	सां	ऽ	नि	म	प
											क्डां	–	धा	धा	धा
												3			
ग	ऽ	मग	मम	रेरे	रेरे	सा	ऽ	सा	सासा	सासा	मम	मऽ	मऽ	पऽ	पऽ
धा	–	क्टि	तक	गदि	गन	धा	ऽ	धा	क्टि	तक	धुम	क्टि	तक	गाद	गन
x				2				0				3			
धऽ	धऽ	धऽ	धऽ	धऽ	धऽ	नि	पऽ	नऽ	रेंऽ	रेंऽ	रेंऽ	रेऽ	रेंऽ	रेंऽ	रेंऽ
गदि	गन	धुम	क्ति	तिक	त्ता	का	क्टि	तक	धुम	क्टि	तक	गदि	गन	नग	तिट
x				2				0				3			
गं	ऽ	ग	ध	ऽ	ध	नि	ऽ	रें	नि	सां	सां	ऽ	नि	म	प
क्डां	ऽ	धा	क्डां	–	धा	क्डां	धा	–	–	–	क्डां	–	धा	धा	धा
x				2				0				3			
ग	ऽ	गऽ	मम	रे	रेऽ	सा	ऽ								
धा	–	क्टि	तक	गदि	गन	धा	–								
x				2											

Antara

म	मम	मम	पप	पप	पप	धध	धध	निऽ	निऽ	निऽ	निऽ	सांऽ	सांनि	सां	सांसां
धा	क्टि	तक	धुम	क्टि	तक	गदि	गन	गदि	गन	धुम	क्टि	तकि	टत	का	क्टि
0				3				x				2			
पऽ	रेंऽ	रेंऽ	रेंऽ	रेंऽ	रेंऽ	रेंऽ	रेंऽ	म	ऽ	म	धऽ	ऽ	ध	नि	ऽ
तक	धुम	क्टि	तक	गदि	गन	नग	तिट	क्डां	-	धा	कडां	-	धा	क्डां	-
0				3				x				2			
नि	सां	ऽ	सां	ऽ	नि	म	प								
धा	-	-	क्डां	-	धा	धा	धा								
0				3											

TRIVAT
Raga Hameer—Ek Taal
Sthayee

सांसा	सासा	सांसां	सांसां	सांसां	सांसां	सा	–	ध	नि	[ग]	[-प]
दिर	दिर	दिर	दिर	दिर	दिर	तों	ऽ	ऽ	ऽ	ऽ	ऽम्
0		3		4		X		0		2	
[म]पप	पप	[प]सां	–	[सां]ध	–	प	प	प	प	प	[प]ग
दिर	दिर	तो	ऽ	म्तो	ऽ	म्त	न	न	न	न	ना
0		3		4		X		0		2	
म	प	प	रे	सा	सा	[नि]सा	सासा	सा	म	ग	पप
ऽ	त	द	रे	दा	नि	ना	दिर	धि	त्ला	ऽ	न्दिर
0		3		4		X		0		2	
पप	[म]प	सां	–	रें	सांसां	सांसां	निनि	धध	निनि	धध	पप
दिर	धि	त्ला	ऽ	दिर	दिर	दिर	दिर	दिर	दिर	दिर	दिर
0		3		4		X		0		2	
[म]पप	पप										
दिर	दिर										
0											

Antara-1

[म]प	प	[प]ग	प	प	प	[नि]सां	ध	सां	–सां	सां	सां
य	ल	लि	य	ल	लि	य	ल	लो	ऽम्	य	ल
X		0		2		0		3		4	
सां	–सां	[नि]सां	[सां]ध	–	सां	सां	रें	[नि]सां	–	सां	ध
लो	ऽम्	य	ला	ऽ	य	ला	ऽ	ल	ऽ	ल्ल	ऽ
X		0		2		0		3		4	

(Contd.)

$^{\text{नि}}$सां	सां	^{ग}मं	$^{\text{मं}}$रें	–	सां	सां	सां	^{ग}मं	रें	सां	सां
दे	रे	ना	दी	ऽ	म्त	दा	नि	त	न	न	न
X		0		2		0		3		4	
ध	प	ग	म	रे	सा	सांसा	सासा				
न	न	न	न	न	न	दिर	दिर				
X				2		0					

Antara-2

^{म}प	ग	^{म}प	प	ध	ध	प	प	$^{\text{नि}}$सां	$^{\text{सां}}$ध	सांसां	सांसां
त	ता	धिं	धिं	थुं	थुं	धिं	धिं	धा	धा	तिर	किट
X		0		2		0		3		4	
संसां	सांसां	सां	सां	–	सांसां	रें	सां	–	सां	^{ध}ध	–
धुम	किट	त	घ्डा	ऽ	न्तक्	धि	त्ला	ऽ	न्त	द्धा	ऽ
X		0		2		0		3		4	
सांसां	–सां	मं	मं	रेंरें	रेंरें	सांसां	सांसां	सां	सां	–	सांसां
चिगि	ऽन्न	धा	धा	तिर	किट	धुम	किट	त	घ्डा	ऽ	न्तक्
X		0		2		0		3		4	
मं	रें	–	सां	ध	–	सां	सां	ध	य	य	ग
धि	त्ला	ऽ	न्त	द्धा	ऽ	धि	त्ला	ऽ	ल्त	द्धा	ऽ
X		0		2		0		3		4	
प	प	–	रे	सा	–	सासा	सासा				
धि	त्ला	ऽ	न्त	द्धा	ऽ	दिर	दिर				
X		0		2		0					

The above Trivat has three parts. The first and the second part are sung with bols of tarana and the third part consists of bols of Pakhawaj. Although the above composition can be termed as Tarana, but Pt. V.N. Bhatkhande has enumerated all the taranas having patas of Pakhawaj into the Trivat category.

TRIVAT
Bhairav–Teen Taal
Sthayee

नि	सां	नि	ध	–	प	(ग)म	ग	म	(नि)ध	–	प	ध	म	प	म
ओ	द	न	तो	ऽ	म्त	न	न	त	दा	ऽ	रे	ता	रे	दा	नि
x				3				0				2			
(ग)म	–	म	रे	ग	म	प	म	(ग)म	–	रे	(ग)रे	–	सा	सा	सा
दी	ऽ	म्त	न	न	न	न	न	ना	ऽ	रे	ना	ऽ	रे	त	न
x				3				0				2			
(म)ग	म	प	प	(प)ग	म	प	ध	नि	सां	नि	ध	प	म	प	ध
नि	ता	ऽ	न्न	तो	ऽ	म्त	दि	या	ना	रे	त	द	रे	त	न
x				3				0				2			

Antara

म	न	प	प	(म)ग	म	(नि)ध	(नि)ध	(नि)ध	(नि)ध	नि	नि	सां	सां	सां	सां
य	ल	ल	मु	य	ल	ल	मु	य	लि	य	ल	ल	ल	ल	ल
0				3				x				2			
(नि)ध	ध	ध	(सां)नि	सां	नि	सां	सां	(ग)रें	–	सां	सां	नि	ध	प	प
य	ल	लि	या	ऽ	ल्ल	ल	ल	लं	ऽ	य	ल	ल	ल	ल	ल
0				3				x				2			
रें	सां	–	नि	धध	पप	गग	मम	पप	पप	(नि)धध	(नि)धध				
तक्	घ्ड़ां	ऽ	तिर	किट	तक	नग	धिर	किट	तक	तक	धिर				
0				3				x							
निनि	सांसां	सां	सां	मं	रें	सां	–	सां	(नि)ध	नि	ध				
किट	तक	तक्	घ्ड़ां	ऽ	तक्	धा	ऽ	तक्	घ्ड़ां	ट	तक्				
2				0				3							
प	–	म	(म)रें	म	रे	सा	–								
धो	ऽ	तक्	घ्ड़ां	ऽ	तक्	धा	ऽ								
0				2											

TRIVAT
Raga–Bhupali–Teen Taal

–	सा	सा	रे	ग	ग	–	ग	–	सा	–	सा	रे	रे	–	सा
	धिरि	किट	तक्	धी	धी	ऽ	–ग	ऽ	धी	ऽ	ना	ती	ती	ऽ	ना
3				X				2				0			
–	सा	–	सा	सा	ग	ग	ग	प	प	प	प	ग	ध	प	प
ऽ	धी	ऽ	–ग	धी	धी	ना	धी	धी	ना	थुं	थुं	ना	थुं	थुं	थुं
3				X				2				0			
ग	रे	सा–	सा–	ग	ग	ग	प	–	ध	सां	सां	प	ध	प	रे
थुं	थुं	किड्	नी	गु	रू	को	गा	ऽ	वे	त	ब	वे	ऽ	द	पा
3				X				2				0			
–	रे	सा	सा	सा	सांऽ	रेऽ	ो	सांऽ	साध	ध	प	गग	पध	धध	पप
ऽ	वे	गु	नी	धिर	किट	तक	धिरि किट तक्	धक्क ड़ां	ऽधा	धा	धा	नग	डझ	गड	तक
ग	रे	–सा	सारे	ग	ग	ऽ	ग								
थुं	ना	ऽधिर	किट तक्	धी	धी		ना								

Antara

ग	–	ग	प	–	प	सां	ध	सां	–	–	सां	–	रे	सां	सां
द्धु	ऽ	त	म	ऽ	घ्य	वि	ऽ	लं	ऽ	ऽ	नी	ऽ	त	औ	र
X				2				0				3			
ध	–	ध	सां	–	रें	सां	सां	ध	–	–	प	–	ध	प	–
ता	ऽ	ल	का	ऽ	ल	स	म	वी	ऽ	ऽ	ज्ञा	ऽ	म	को	ऽ
X				2				0				3			

(Contd.)

गं	–	रें	ग	·गं	रें	सां	सां	ध	ध	–	प	ग	ग	प	ध
वं	ऽ	ठ	ब	र	न	क	र	दि	खा	ऽ	वे	सु	ध	म	त
x				2				0				3			
सां	सां	ध	प	ग	–	रे	ग	–	–	सा	रे	–	सा	–	–
त	ब	ब	डो	गा	ऽ	य	क	ऽ	ऽ	क	हा	ऽ	वे	ऽ	ऽ
x				2				0				3			
–	रे	सा	सा	सा	सांऽ	रेऽ	सां	सांऽ	साध	ध	प	गग	पध	धध	पप
ऽ	वे	गु	नी	धिर	किट	तक	धिरि किट तक्	धक ड़ां	ऽधा	धा	धा	नग	डझ	गड	तक
ग	रे	–सा	सारे	ग	ग	ऽ	ग								
थुं	ना	ऽधिर	किट तक्	धी	धी		ना								

RAAGMALA
Tala – Dhamar

Sthayee

													रें सा
सं	–	नि	नि	सां	सां	–	नि	–	प	–	म	–	–
–	–	रं	ग	न	य	–	नी	–	–	–	का	–	–
3					x				2		0		
प	–	प	–	नि	प	–	म	–	रे	स	रे	स	रे
हे	–	को	–	कि	यौ	–	ए	–	तो	–	मा	न	सा
3				x					2		0		

Antara

रें	–	–	रें	–	–	गं	रें	–	–	सां	–	–	नि
गो	–	–	री	–	–	ग	हे	–	–	रू	–	–	छा
x					2		0			3			
रें	–	–	रें	–	–	गं	रें	–	–	सां	–	–	–
ड	–	–	मि	–	–	लि	ला	–	–	ले	–	–	–
x					2		0			3			
मं	मं	–	ग	–	ग	–	मं	ध	–	नि	–	–	–
म	न	–	क्र	–	म	–	व	च	–	न	–	–	–
x					2		0			3			
सां	–	–	नि	–	ध	–	प	–	–	मं	–	ग	–
या	–	–	तें	–	–	–	हो	–	–	त	–	क	–
x					2		0			3			
प	–	–	रे	–	–	–	स	–	रे	सां	–	नि	नि
ल्या	–	–	–	–	–	–	न	–	सा	–	–	रं	ग
x					2		0			3			

Sanchari

म	नि	–	ध	–	प	–	प	प	–	रे	–	–	रे
जि	प	–	ह	–	ठ	–	क	रे	–	री	–	–	तू
x					2		0			3			
रे	ग	–	ग	म	प	–	ग	म	रे	स	–	स	–
न	ट	–	ना	–	–	–	ग	र	–	सौ	–	–	–
x					2		0			3			
ध	–	–	प	–	म	ग	रे	–	–	ग	म	प	म
भैं	–	–	रौ	–	–	–	ही	–	–	दे	–	व	–
x					2		0			3			
रे	–	–	–	–	–	–	स	–	–	–	–	–	–
गा	–	–	–	–	–	–	न	–	–	–	–	–	–
x					2		0			3			

Abhogi

नि	ध	–	नि	–	–	–	सां	–	–	सां	–	–	नि
मु	र	–	ली	–	–	–	ता	–	–	न	–	–	का
x					2		0			3			
–	ध	–	सां	–	रे	–	गं	–	–	रे	–	सां	–
–	न्ह	रौ	–	–	–	गा	–	–	व	–	–	त	–
x					2		0			3			
नि	नि	प	ध	–	म	–	प	–	–	पध	मप	सां	–
सु	न	–	लै	–	–	–	री	–	–	हां-	--	हां	–
x					2		0			3			
नि	नि	प	ध	–	म	–	प	–	–	सां	–	रे	–
सु	न	–	लै	–	–	–	री	–	–	दै	–	–	–
x					2		0			3			

(Contd.)

गं	–	–	रे	सां	निध	पध	नि	धम	रे	सां	–	नि	नि
का	–	–	–	–	–	–	–	न–	–	सा	–	रं	ग

Sanchari

रे	ग	–	स	–	रे	रे	प	–	–	ध	–	–	–
रं	–	–	ग	–	–	रं	गी	–	–	ली	–	–	–
x					2		0			3			
म	म	–	प	–	–	ध	सां	सां	–	निध	पध	नि	धम
सु	ध	–	र	–	–	ना	–	य	–	की-	--	–	--
x					2		0			3			
रे	–	–	रें	–	सां	–	सां	–	–	ध	–	–	नि
तू	–	–	जि	–	य	–	में	–	–	–	–	–	अ
x					2		0			3			
सां	–	–	ध	–	नि	प	ग	म	–	रे	–	स	–
ड़ा	–	–	–	–	–	–	–	–	–	न	–	–	–
x					2		0			3			

Abhogi

प	–	–	सां	–	–	सां	सां	सां	–	सां	–	7	नि
नं	–	–	द	–	–	दा	–	स	–	के	–	–	–
x					2		0			3			
ध	–	–	प	–	–	–	'म	प	ध	म	–	(ग)प	–
दा	–	–	रौ	–	–	–	क	रि	–	कें	–	–	–
x					2		0			3			
नि	स	–	ग	–	–	म	प	–	प	नि	–	नि	–
यौं	–	–	ही	–	–	वि	हा	–	य	ग	–	यौ	–
x					2		0			3			
सां	–	नि	प	–	–	–	गम	ग	रे	स	–	नि	नि
मा	–	–	–	–	–	–	न–	–	सा	–	–	रें	ग
x					2		0			3			

This Raag Mala is sung in Haveli Sangeet tradition. It is composed in Ragas—Sarang, Gauri, Kalyan, Nata, Bhairav, Kanhara, Nayaki and Adana. In the note combinations नि प म रे, रे ग रे सानि, प मं ग प रे, रें रें सां ध नि सां ध नि प the ragas—Sarang, Gauri, Kalyan, Adana respectively are very distinctly presented. This is a rare composition in the style of Dhrupad.

Raga Sagar—Ek Tala (Vilambit)

छाय रही बहार निज भूपतिलक की ।।ध०।।
सोहनी सूरत मनोहरी मूरत दरबार में सोहे जेसे शाम की।।

प	रे	रेग	ममप	म	ग	रे	–ग	[म]प	–	निनिपमप	मगममप
छा	ऽ	यऽ	ऽऽर	ही	ऽ	ऽ	ऽव	हा	ऽ	ऽऽऽऽऽ	ऽऽरनिज
3		4		X		0		2		0	
प	–	ध	पध	पध	पध-पध	गप	गरे	म	ग	सारेग	निसासासा
भू	ऽ	ऽ	ऽ	पऽ	ऽऽऽ-ऽऽऽ	ऽऽ	ऽऽ	ती	ऽ	ऽऽऽ	लककीऽ
3		4		X		0		2		0	

अंतरा

ग	,मंध	निसां-	निसों	सां-सां	रें गं	रें गं	रें	सा-	सारेंध	सांध
सो	,हनि	सूऽ	ऽऽऽऽर	तऽम	नोऽ	ऽ ऽ	ह्	रीऽ	मूऽऽ	ऽर
3		4		X	0		2		0	
सां	–,सारें	गं–	[म]गं,रें गं	–रेंरेंसांनि	धनिसारें	रेसां	सां–	निसां	निरें	[ध]निमंप
त	ऽ,दर	बाऽऽऽ,	ऽऽ	रऽऽऽ	ऽऽऽऽ	मेऽ	सोऽ	ऽहे	जैऽ	ऽऽसे
3		4		X	0		2		0	
मरे	नि[म]सा	रेग	गमपप		म					
श्याऽ मकी		छाऽ	यऽऽर		ही					
3		4			X					

Raga Sagar—Teen Tala

मनोहरी जनरंजनी जग मोहनी हास्य निधानो ।। धृ।।
हरीप्रिय कीर्ति तुभ्फो देशि चिलसे रवि पूर्एचंद्रिके-
विपाही शंकर सम भुवनी।

स्थायी

प	नि	–	(प)नि	सां	–	–	म	रे	ग	रे	ग	रे	सा	–	म
न	रं	ऽ	ज	नी	ऽ	ऽ	म	नो	ऽ	ऽ	ऽ	ह	री	ऽ	ज
3				x				2				0			

प	मप	नि	(प)नि	सां	–	निसां	प	नि	सां	रें	सां	नि	–	–	प
न	रंऽ	ऽ	ज	नी	ऽ	ऽऽ	ज	ग	मो	ऽ	ह	नी	ऽ	ऽ	ऽ
3				x				2				0			

गम	पनि	प	पम	ग	–	सा	म	ग	रे	रे	ग	रे	सा	–	म
हाऽ	ऽऽ	स्य	निऽ	धा	ऽ	नी	म	नो	ऽ	ऽ	ऽ	ह	री	ऽ,	ज
3				x				2				0			

अंतरा

म प नि – – – – –, निनि सां – – निसां निसारें मंगरेसां निसां-
ह री ऽऽ ऽऽऽऽ, प्रिय की ऽ ऽ ऽऽ ऽऽऽऽऽऽतिं तुभ्फीऽ
0 3 x 2

रें	–	–	प	मं रें		गं रें	सां	(प)सां	रें	सारें	गंगरें रेंसा	नि	सां	सां	निसां
दे	ऽ	ऽ	ऽ	ऽऽऽ	ऽशि		वि	ल	ऽ	ऽऽ	ऽऽऽ ऽऽ	ऽ	ऽ	से	ऽऽ
0				3				x				2			

प	प	नि	–	प	नि	–	सां	नि	–	प	म	–	–,प	नि	नि
र	चि	पृ	ऽ	र्ए	चं	ऽ	द्रि	के	ऽ	ऽ	चि	ऽ	ऽ,पा	ऽ	हि
0				3				x				2			

नि	ध	(सां)	सां	(प)	–	गग^{प}	प	^{प}ग	–	सा	म	ग	रे	रे	^{म}ग
शं	ऽ	ऽ	क	र	ऽ	सम्म	भु	व	ऽ	नि	म	नो	ऽ	ऽ	ऽ
0				3								2			
रे	सा	–	म												
ह	री	ऽ	ज												
0															

Raga Sagar – Teen Tala

काहे तोडी प्रति मालनिया, विभस भये प्रीत तिहारे
तुमहो चतुर सुधर अलवेलरिया
धन धन धन, सुहागनिया, मालनिया।

अंतरा

तुमहो भवानी भैरवी समानी, सारंग नयनी
गौर सारंग रंगनीया, मालनिया।[4]

स्थायी

															ध
															कां
नि़	सा	–	रे	ग	–	–	ग	सा	रे	सारे	ग	रे	रे	सा,	सा
हे	तो	ऽ	डि	प्री	ऽ	ऽ	त	भा	ऽ	ऽऽ	ऽ	ल	नि	या,	वि
3				X				2				0			
ध	ध	–	ध	प	–	–	–	ग	प	ध	प	ग	रे	सा,	सा
भ	स	ऽ	भ	ये	ऽ	ऽ	ऽ	प्री	ऽ	त	ति	हा	ऽ	रे	तु
3				X				2				0			
नि	नि	–	प	म	म	–	म	म	म	म	म	नी	–	पम	प
म	हा	ऽ	च	तु	र	ऽ	सु	ध	र	अ	ल	बे	ऽ	लऽ	रि
3				X				2				0			
ग	–	म	नि	प	सां	–	नि	सां	–	सां	–	–	–	–	सां
या	ऽ	ऽ	न	ध	ऽ	न	ध	ऽ	न	ऽ	ऽ	ऽ	ऽ	ऽ	सु
3				X				2				0			
नि	नि	पम	रेसा–रे	ग	–	–	–	सा	रे	सारे	ग	रे	रे	सा,	ध
हा	ऽ	ऽऽ	ऽऽग	नी	ऽ	ऽ	ऽ	मा	ऽ	ऽऽ	ऽ	ल	नि	या,	का
3				X				2				0			

अंतरा

														म॑	
प	ध	नि	ध	म॑	–	ग	–	–	–	सां	–	सां	सां–	रें	तु
म	हो	ऽ	भ	वा	ऽ	नी	ऽ	ऽ	ऽ	भे	ऽ	र	वि	ऽ	स
3				x				2				0			
सां	–	–	–	रें	–	सां	–	–	–	–	सां	–	नि	–	प
मा	ऽ	ऽ	ऽ	ऽ	ऽ	नो,	ऽ	ऽ	ऽ	ऽ	सा	ऽ	रं	ऽ	ग
3				x				2				0			
म	पम	रे	–	–	–	–	ग	–	ग	ग	–	ग	--	ग,	ग
न	यऽ	नी	ऽ	ऽ	ऽ	ऽ	गो	ऽ	र	सा	ऽ	रं	अ	ग	रं
3				x				2				0			
–	म	ग	रे	म	ग	प	रे	सा	–	सारे	ग	रे	रे	सा,	ध
ऽ	ग	नी	ऽ	ऽ	ऽ	ऽ	ऽ	या	ऽ	माऽ	ऽ	ल	नि	या,	का
3				x				2				0			

BAMANI SARGAM
Raga Yaman—Teen Tala

निरगमधन मांगोरो सुरस, नंद्नंदन सरग मगरस,
निरगम पदपे नाद परोसो ।।धृ।।
पाप पदनपे, धन सरननमे मननिस सुरसो,
धुनसुरननभो, गीर गीर मेरी पैर परीसो।।[5]

नि	रे	ग	म॑	ध	नि	म	–	गा	–	रे	–	स	रे	स	–
नि़	र	ग	म	ध	न	मां	ऽ	गो	ऽ	री	ऽ	सु	र	स	ऽ
0				3				x				2			

नि	–	ध	नि	–	ध	नि	–	स	रे	ग	म	ग	रे	स	–
नं	ऽ	द	न	ऽ	द	न	ऽ	स	र	ग	म	ग	र	स	ऽ
0				3				x				2			

नि	रे	ग	म	प	ध	प	–	नि	–	ध	प	रे	–	स	–
नि़	र	ग	म	प	द	पे	ऽ	ना	ऽ	द	प	रो	ऽ	सो	ऽ
0				3				x				2			

प	–	प	प	ध	नि	प	–	ध	नि	स	रे	नि	नि	म	–
पा	ऽ	प	प	द	न	पे	ऽ	ध	न	स	र	न	न	मे	ऽ
0				3				x				2			

म	नि	नि	स	स	रे	स	–	ध	नि	स	रे	नि	नि	म	–
म	न	नि	स	सु	र	सो	ऽ	धु	न	सु	र	न	न	मो	ऽ
0				3				x				2			

ग	–	रे	ग	–	रे	म	रे	ध	–	रे	प	रे	–	स	–
गी	ऽ	र	गी	ऽ	र	मे	री	दे	ऽ	र	प	री	ऽ	सा	ऽ
0				3				x				2			

BAMANI SARGAM
Raga–Bhupali–Teen Taal

गिरधर सिर गगरी गिरपरे।
सिरपर गगरी पग परू सारे।। धृ।।
पग धर सारे गगरि सिरधारे
गिर गिर राग पराग परू सारे।।[6]

ग	रे	ध़	रे	स	रे	ग	ग	री	–	–	ग	रे	प	रे	–
गि	र	ध	र	सि	र	ग	ग	री	ऽ	ऽ	गि	र	प	रे	ऽ
0				3				X				2			
स	रे	प	रे	ग	ग	रे	–	प	ग	प	रे	स	–	रे	–
सि	र	प	र	ग	ग	री	ऽ	प	ग	प	रूँ	सा	ऽ	रे	ऽ
0				3				X				2			
प	ग	ध	रे	स	–	रे	–	ग	ग	रे	स	रे	ध	–	रे
प	ग	ध	र	सा	ऽ	रे	ऽ	ग	ग	रि	सि	र	धा	ऽ	रे
0				3				X				2			
ग	रे	ग	रे	रे	–	ग	प	रे	–	ग	प	रे	स	–	रे
गि	र	गि	र	रा	ऽ	ग	प	रा	ऽ	ग	प	रूं	सा	ऽ	रे
0				3				X				2			

REFERENCES

1. Collection of Rajabhaiya Poochwale by Dr. Prabhakar Narayan Chinchore, p. 22.
2. Acquired from Prof. R.S. Bisht.
3. Agra Gharana Gayaki Aur Chhije, Ramanlal Mehta, pp. 14-15.
4. Raga Sumanmala, p. 141.
5. Raga Sumanmala, pp. 145-46.
6. Raga Sumanmala, pp. 143-44.

Conclusion

In the foregoing chapters, an attempt has been made to analyze some of the lesser known forms of Hindustani Classical music. The study included Chaturang, Trivat, Raag Mala or Raga Sagar and Bamani Sargam or Svarsagar.

The first chapter traces the evolution of compositional forms and shows how our musical tradition, in spite of the several modifications and adjustments during the course of the centuries have been maintained in essence throughout. Earliest references to compositions are found in the Vedas. The five fold divisions of the Saman (Prastav, Udgith, Pratihara, Upadrav and Nidhan), provides the basic for the structure of the later Prabandha and Dhruvapada forms consisting mainly of Udgraha, Dhruva, Melapak, Antara and Abhoga.

Although the foreign elements entered into the stream of Hindustani Classical music, the origin of the compositional forms like Dhrupad and Khayal could be traced back to the Prabandhas.

The first chapter is the elaborate study of the compositional forms from the time of the Vedas till date.

Besides, the compositional forms which were discussed in chapter one, there are other forms of Hindustani Classical music, which are lesser known today. In the second chapter the historical perspective of the lesser known forms were studied. The forms included–Chaturang, Trivat, Raag Mala and Bamani Sargam. After a scientific study it was established that these forms had their root in the Prabandhas. Matanga in his Brihaddeshi has mentioned about Chaturang Prabandha. Besides this many Prabandhas were found in different treatises of music which resemble the forms, Chaturang, Trivat, Raag Mala, Bamani Sargam etc.

Mention of the forms like Chaturang, Trivat, Ragasagar were found in the compositions of the great composers like Tansen, Baiju, Gopal Nayak etc.

In the third chapter it was my endeavour to present a full-fledged study of the lesser known forms from the point of view of present day performance. Although these forms are rarely heard today, this researcher was able to collect some compositions from different artistes of different gharana. The forms Chaturang, Trivat, Raag Mala and Bamani Sargam are still in practice among the artistes of different gharanas like Gwalior, Agra, Delhi etc. The lesser known forms also prevail in Vaishnav music and Sufi music. For example, in Haveli Sangeet Parampara, compositions resembling Chaturang, Trivat and Raag Mala are still sung.

The fourth chapter deals with the prospects and problems of preservation of the lesser known forms. I tried to provide some suggestions for preservation of the lesser known forms. For example, Chaturang, Trivat etc., can be used as the ending piece in a concert like Thumri, Tappa and Bhajan etc.

This researcher has collected many compositions of the lesser known forms from different artistes of various gharanas and also from various authoritative books. The compositions with notation have been given in the fifth chapter.

Bibliography

ENGLISH

A Historical Study of Indian Music, Swami Prajnananandaw, Anandadhara Prakashan, Calcutta, 1948.

A History of Indian Literature, M.Winternitz, University of Calcutta, Vol.I, Pt-I.

Ain-i-Akbari, Abul Fazl, Allami, Vol.III, English Translation by H S Jarret, Royal Asiastic Society, Calcutta, 1948.

Ain-i-Akbari, Abul Fazl, English translation by H Blochmann, New Imperial Book Depot, New Delhi.

Aspects of Indian Music, edited by Dr Sumati Mutatkar, Sangeet Natak Academi, 1987.

Brihaddeshi of Shri Matanga Muni, Edited by Dr Prem Lata Sharma, Indira Gandhi National Centre for the Arts, 1992.

Dhrupada, Indurana Srivastava, Motilal Banarasidass, Delhi 1980.

Evolution of Khayal, M.V. Dhond, Sangeet Natak Academi.

Evolution of Raga and Tala, M.R. Gautam, Munshiram Manoharlal Publishers, Delhi 1989.

Hindustani Music, Dr. Najma Perveen Ahmad, Manohar Publications, New Delhi, 1980.

Historical Development of Indian Music, Swami Prajnanananda, Pub. K.L. Mukhopadhayay, Calcutta, 1960, 1973.

Sacred Symphony, Dr. (Ms.) Krishna Bisht, Bhagirath Sewa Sansthan, Ghaziabad, 1986.

Sangeet Ratnakar, Vol. I and II English translation 1989, Dr R K Shringy and Dr. P L Sharma, Munshiram Manoharlal Publishers, Delhi.

Significance of Compositional forms in Hindustani Music, Dr. Manjushree Tyagi.

Time Measure and Compositional Types in Indian Music, Dr. Subhadra Chaudhuri, Aditya Prakashan, New Delhi, 1997.

HINDI

Agra Gharana, Parampara Gayaki aur Cheeje, Raman Lal Mehta, Maharaja Vishvavidylaya, Baroda, 1969.

Bhartiya Sangeet Ka Itihas, S.S. Paranjape, Chowkhamba Banaras, 1969.

Dhruvapada Aur Uska Vikas, Acharya Brihaspati, Bihar Rashtrabhasha Parishad, 1951.

Kramik Pustak Malika, Pt.V.N.Bhatkhande, Sangeet Karyalaya, Hathras, Part-I to VI.

Man Singh aur Mankutuhal, H.N.Dwivedi, Gwalior, Samrat 2010, 1st ed.

Najo of Wajid Ali Shah, translated into Hindi Yogesh Praveen, U.P. Sangeet Natak Academy, 1989.

Pushtimargiya Mandiron ki Sangeet Parampara, Prof. Satyabhan Sharma, Radha Publications, 1999.

Raga Suman Mala of Balabhan Umdekar, edited by Sangeeta Kanthale, Madhya Pradesh Hindi Grantha Academy, 1989.

Raga Vigyan, V.R. Patvardhan, Sangeet Gourav Grantha Mala, Pune.

Sahasras, edited by Dr. P. L. Sharma, Sangeet Natak Academy, New Delhi, 1972.

Sangeet Bhashya, S. Bandopadhya, B R Publishing Corporation, Delhi.

SANSKRIT

Bharat Kosha, Ramakrishna Kavi, Tirupati, 1951.

Brihaddeshi, Matang Muni, Trivandrum Sanskrit Series, 1928.

Chaturdandi Prakashika, Pt.Venkatmakhin, Madras Music Academy, 1934.

Manasollasa, Someshvara, Gaekwad's oriental series, Baroda 1961.

Natya Shastra (Kasi edition)

Sangeet Darpan, Damodar, Sangeet Karyalaya, Hathras.

Sangeet Raj, edited by Dr. Premlata Sharma, Hindu Vishvavidyalaya Sanskrit Sangeet Mala, 1963.

Sangeet Samayasara, Parshvadeva, Trivandrum Sanskrit series 1925.

JOURNALS AND PAPERS

Sangeet Research Academy, Vol.8, No.1, August 1987.

Commemoration volume in honour of Dr. S. N. Ratanjankar, 1961.

Dhrupad Annual, 1986, 87, 88, 89.

Index